BOOKS BY HELEN HILL MILLER

Sicily and the Western Colonies of Greece

Greece • A WORLD BACKGROUND BOOK

Greek Horizons

SICILY AND THE WESTERN COLONIES OF GREECE

Helen Hill Miller

SICILY

AND THE WESTERN COLONIES OF GREECE

Charles Scribner's Sons · New York

Copyright © 1965 HELEN HILL MILLER

Grateful acknowledgment is made to the following copyright owners for permission to quote as indicated:

CAMBRIDGE UNIVERSITY PRESS, Theocritus *Idylls* tr. A. S. F. Gow; DOUBLEDAY & Co., INC. and WILLIAM HEINEMANN, LTD. (London): Homer *The Odyssey* tr. Robert Fitzgerald; DOUBLEDAY & Co., INC. and C. DAY LEWIS: Virgil's *Eclogues and Georgics;* E. P. DUTTON & Co., INC. and J. M. DENT AND SONS, LTD. (London): Herodotus *History* tr. George Rawlinson, Everyman's Library; HARVARD UNIVERSITY PRESS, Diodorus Siculus *Library of History,* Strabo *Geography,* Polybius *Histories,* Cicero *Orations,* Ovid *Tristia,* Loeb Classical Library; HAROLD MATSON COMPANY, INC. Virgil *The Aeneid,* tr. C. Day Lewis (Copyright 1952 by C. DAY LEWIS); NEW DIRECTIONS, Pindar *1st Pythian Ode* tr. Richmond Lattimore; L. ARNOLD POST: Plato *Letters;* RANDOM HOUSE, INC. and WILLIAM COLLINS & Co., LTD. (London): Goethe *Italian Journey* tr. W. H. Auden and Elizabeth Mayer; UNIVERSITY OF CHICAGO PRESS: Pindar *Odes tr.* Richmond Lattimore.

A-10.65 [UJ]

Library of Congress Catalog Card Number 65-27243

CONTENTS

SICILY AND THE WESTERN COLONIES OF GREECE

On Names, Places, Sources

To write about Magna Graecia, the area in Southern Italy and Sicily that the city states of the Greek peninsula and the Aegean colonized in their outthrust to the west, is to encounter, open-eyed, a number of special difficulties.

The modern world takes easily to the air—the legendary flight of Daedalus from Crete to Sicily seems wholly natural. But that same world, when on the ground, thinks of surface travel as travel overland. To travel by ship is to go the slow way; seas are thought to divide land from land; streams are one more river to cross.

Such habits of thought are poor preparation for following the Greeks overseas to Magna Graecia. The land these colonists knew $\qquad$ 11 at home and the land that they found in Southern Italy and Sicily was formidably mountainous. Their fast transport was in swift ships over the wine-dark sea. River-mouths made snug harbors. Mainland Greece and the Peloponnese were connected only by the slender (and brigand-infested) Isthmus of Corinth; between the Italian and the Sicilian areas of settlement the Straits of Messina were narrow. Colonization on, or only slightly inland from the coast was the common characteristic of both the parent and the newly approached peninsula.

While sporadic emigration invested shores as far away in the western Mediterranean as Gaul and Spain, most of the western outthrust of the Greeks was highly concentrated. Beginning at Taranto, inside the heel of the Italian boot, the city states of Greece planted offshoots in close proximity to each other around instep and toe, and on up the west coast of the peninsula as far as Cumae, just north of Naples. They occupied all the good sites on the eastern shore of Sicily, and placed fewer but powerful settlements on the south coast as far west as Selinunte, and sporadic outposts on the north coast as far west as Himera.

Identification of these cities presents not only the persistent problem of the spelling of Greek proper names anywhere, but one doubled by the fact that many cities, over the centuries of the classical world, successively bore both Greek and Roman names, with some known today by the former, some by the latter, and some by subsequent Arabic or Italian variants.

Akragas of the Greeks became the Romans' Agrigentum, the Arabs' Girgenti, today's Agrigento. Selinus and Solus became Selinunte and Solunte. Tauromenium is Taormina. Kymai is Cumae; Poseidonia, Paestum; Catana, Catania. Lilybaeum replaced Motya, and the Arabs renamed it Marsala—the harbor of Allah. Parthenope, renamed Neapolis by the Greeks themselves, is Naples.

I have spinelessly abandoned the problem unsolved. The maps on pages 14–15 should help. In the text, I start with the original name of a city; thereafter, I frequently use its best-known counterpart. Yet such cowardice is not particularly rewarding: the quotations I cite have their own spelling systems.

The difficulties created by double names are not confined to places. The gods of the Greeks and those of the Romans corresponded closely in personality, predilection and power—but not in name. Zeus became Jupiter; Hera, Juno; Demeter, Ceres; Aphrodite, Venus; Hermes, Mercury; Artemis, Diana.

Odysseus (Ulysses, to the Romans) and Aeneas both met adventures, overseen—and indeed often occasioned—by the same deities and at the same places in Southern Italy and Sicily, but Homer calls the gods by Greek names, Vergil, by Latin. Text and quotations must be read mindful of these unavoidable discrepancies.

For geographical convenience in planning an itinerary, an enumeration of the sequence of places around the Italian and Sicilian coasts may be of service, particularly because no such tidy pattern emerges when attention is given to the Greek provenance of the new settlements, to the racial strains from which the settlers came, or to the criss-crossed lines of alliance that determined their later history. The modern names are used.

Starting from Cumae, just north of Naples, and with * indicating ancient Greek cities whose modern remains are scanty, the chief sites down the west coast of Italy are Naples, Paestum, Velia, Vibo Valentia (Hipponium), Rosarno (Medma*—its many statues are in the Reggio Museum), the rock of Scilla and Reggio di Calabria at the Straits. Greek artifacts exist elsewhere: Pompeii is Roman, but there are ruins from the days when it was held by Hellenized Samnites; Herculaneum counted Herakles himself as its founder.

13

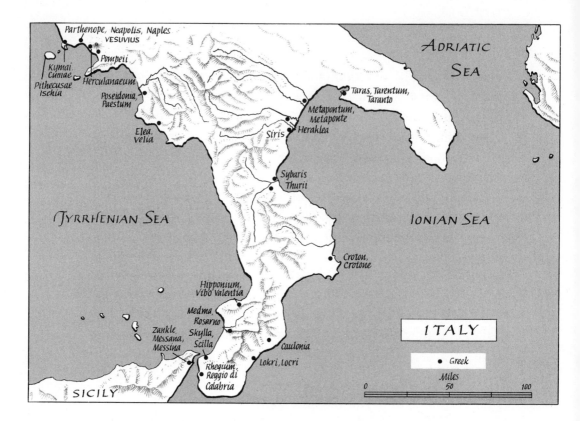

Around the toe of the boot beyond Reggio di Calabria along the south coast are the sites of Lokri, Caulonia*, Crotone*, Sybaris-Thurii*, Siris*, Heraklea Metaponte, Taranto.

In Sicily, Messina lies across the Straits from Reggio. West of it on the north coast are the Greek sites of Milazzo, Tyndari, Himera, and Roman Solunte. South of it on the east coast are Taormina, Naxos, Catania, Leontini*, Megara Hyblaea, Syracuse. The chief south coast sites are Gela, Agrigento, Heraclea Minoa, Selinunte, with Palazzo Acreide slightly inland.

In Sicily, two groups of non-Greek sites need also to be noted; like the Etruscan cities north of Rome they are relevant to the great days of the western Greeks. In the interior of the island the

14

Sicilian aborigines maintained a Hellenized culture that produced great artifacts—at Enna in the east-central section, Centuripe northeast of it towards Mount Aetna, Morgantina southeast of it near Aidone, Segesta in the far northwest. The evidence of recent excavations in the new museum at Caltanissetta shows how deeply Greek influence penetrated these fastnesses.

Arcing around the northwest of the island are the Punic settlements. The Phoenicians moved west slightly in advance of the Greeks. Intrepid sailors, they planted Carthage to dominate North Africa, and other colonies on the shores of both Africa and Spain, even on the Atlantic coast beyond the Pillars of Hercules. No less tenacious than the Greeks of eastern Sicily, Punic settlers, chiefly from Carthage, held the west coast of the island from Marsala to Trapani and the north coast from Erice as far east as Palermo and Solunte.

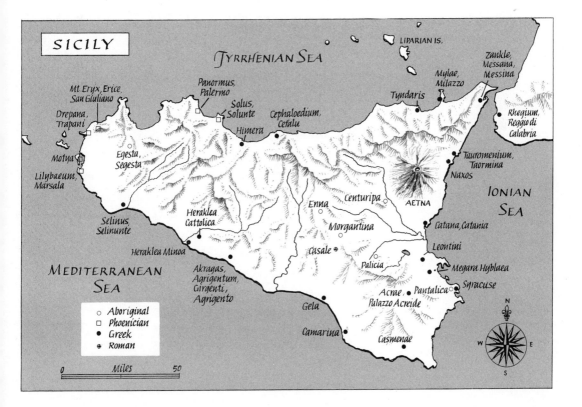

On Names, Places, Sources

The traveller who reaches Sicily by rail from Rome or Naples, crossing the Straits on the train ferry from Villa San Giovanni to Messina, or who flies from Naples to Catania, enters Greek Sicily. The traveller who takes the overnight boat from Naples to Palermo leaves, perhaps with the moon over Vesuvius and Capri, a harbor that was once Greek, but when daylight slants through his porthole, the ship, with Monte Pellegrino on the west, will be nosing into the magnificent Carthaginian roadstead of the Sicilian capital. If he comes this way by air, his plane will likewise touch down on Punic territory, either at Palermo or Trapani.

With Naples or Palermo as convenient but by no means exclusive starting points, considerable choice is available among ways to see the ancient sites. Pullman tour buses, with guides and with hotel accommodations assured, are available—in Sicily, one such tour makes a round of the island visiting major coastal points with a five-day itinerary. Private cars, with or without driver and guide, may be hired; main roads are both well-surfaced and well-marked; modern motels are available in major centers.

My own method was a combination of foot and rail: I took the train to the nearest station, left my simple luggage there, and walked to my chosen destination. The compact, Diesel-driven Sicilian trains are frequent and clean; they leave not only on time but often two or three minutes in advance of schedule. And where trains don't run, or where, as in the center of the island at Enna, the mountains are such as to give pause even to the little engine that could, a bus will be there to climb the rest of the way.

My system was delightfully flexible. I went to a site and stayed until I was ready to leave. In precious solitude, I could outwait the tourist with an enforced time-table, lunch in the open on bread and cheese, form my own impressions at my own rate, wait for sunlight to brighten stone and blacken shadow. (My cameras are Heiland Pentaxes with .35 and 1.35 lenses. Some illustrations are from black and white film shot at double its ASA rating; others are converted from color.)

Either before I came, or on site with paperbacks of the classics in my pocket, I read my way beyond need of an ordinary guide or a Muirhead-Hachette-Baedeker handbook.

The list of contemporary books on Greek Sicily and Southern Italy is not nearly as long as that on Greece and its islands. Leonard von Matt's *Ancient Sicily* and *Magna Graecia* contain superb pictures of sites, coins, statues and vases representative of the entire area. A. G. Woodhead's *The Greeks in the West,* a compact summary of the archaeologist's Magna Graecia, available in paperback, is an indispensable companion; in the same series is Donald Harden's *The Phoenicians.* Both have maps, chronologies, drawings, pictures, bibliographies. Among rare books, the four volumes of J. Houel's *Voyage pittoresque des îles de Sicile, de Malte et de Lipari,* Paris, 1782–87, with large engravings, show the sites as they were before archaeology.

But ancient writers are the really rewarding sources for the feeling that goes with fact. Homer, Hesiod, Vergil are incomparable raconteurs for an evening of prehistory. Choice of translations of the *Odyssey* ranges happily from Chapman to Rieu. Richmond Lattimore has just translated the *Theogony.* Discontent with the *Aeneid* in English oscillates between the blandness of Rolfe Humphries and the sometimes exuberant heartiness of C. Day Lewis.

Many of Pindar's *Odes,* now available in Lattimore translations, were composed under the patronage of the great Sicilian tyrants; he, Simonides and Bacchylides all graced their courts. Aeschylus wrote his *Aetnaeans* and staged his *Persians* for command performances at Syracuse. Euripides' *Cyclops* buffoons Odysseus' encounter at the foot of Aetna. Plato's efforts to turn a Sicilian tyrant into a philosopher-king are the subject of many of his extant *Letters,* and philosophers and rhetoricians from Magna Graecia—Gorgias, Parmenides—are persons in his *Dialogues.* In the Indian summer of Greek Sicily, Theocritus wrote his *Pastorals,* contemporary with Archimedes' major discoveries in science and mathematics at Syracuse.

Later Roman writers preserved much from now-lost Greek sources. Plutarch's *Lives* include such personnages related to the history of Magna Graecia as Nicias and Alcibiades, Dion and Timoleon, Pyrrhus and Marcellus.

Cicero's *Verrine Orations* are a veritable catalogue of the art of Greek Sicily. The Greek Baedeker of the second century A.D., Pausanias, enumerates the Magna Graecian votives erected in honor of athletic or military victories at Olympia and Delphi and still extant in his time.

Among historians, Diodorus Siculus in the first century B.C. collected data from many previous writers, including fragments from more contemporary chroniclers such as Philistus and Timaeus whose works are lost. Strabo, Pliny and Polybius record events of the Greek centuries.

But for the periods which they treat, the sources of all sources are Herodotus and Thucydides. The former describes the battle of Himera with the same zest as Marathon, Thermopylae and Salamis. The latter is a still-respected authority for the dates of colonization in the west, and he was a contemporary observer of the contest between Athens and Syracuse.

CHAPTER I

The Power of Typhoes

Sweeping across the Mediterranean on a flight into or out of Rome, few travellers have failed to startle at the sudden sight, through a south window as their plane crossed the boot of Italy, of a lonely eminence that confronts passing aircraft at a height comparable to their own.

Sometimes it is a grey, white-tipped triangle above an indeterminate bank of cloud or mist, abstract form superimposed on shapelessness. Sometimes it is a solid, three-dimensional cone, broadly-based on a visible island. But whatever its manifestation of the moment, century after century new arrivals have viewed this mountain with awe.

The Greeks called it Aetna. Their successors gave it a compound name, Mongibello, from the Latin *mons* and the Arabic *djebel*. Both words mean mountain, and mountain of mountains indeed it is.

At airplane cruising speeds, the sight is quickly gone. To travellers with far destinations, it is an incident in a long journey. But travellers bent on visiting the areas of classical Greek migration and colonization in the western Mediterranean, the sites of the centuries when much of Southern Italy and more than half of Sicily were known as Magna Graecia, should begin their orientation here.

If, in a helicopter, one could hover at Aetna's height above the Straits of Messina, the significance of the coasts below would be far easier to grasp than when they are approached with earth-bound limits of vision at ground or sea level. There aloft, with the boot of Italy from heel to toe and the island of Sicily—forever just escaping the toe's pointed kick—comprised in one far-sweeping overview, a series of overlays on this outspread map could do much to render the coming journey intelligible.

The first overlay, at this godlike height, might appropriately identify the locations associated with the Olympians. In Greece itself, certain places were the preferred sanctuaries of certain deities. Mount Olympos was their shared citadel. Crete was the birthplace and childhood home of Zeus. The island of Delos was the birthplace of the twins, Artemis and Apollo. Delphi was Apollo's amphitheater. Eleusis celebrated the mysteries of Demeter and Persephone.

So also in Magna Graecia. Apollo's voice was heard again in the shrine of the Cumaean Sibyl. In Sicily, a connected group of myths explains both the power of Mount Aetna in the northeast of the island and the countervailing but lesser power of Mount

Eryx in the northwest—powers that tore and divided Sicily throughout the Greek period.

The island is in the form of a triangle. Indeed, its early name was Trinacria, from the three points, Peloros in the northeast, Pachinos in the southeast and Eryx in the northwest, that define its shape. The Trinacrian symbol, dating back at least to its appearance on fourth century Syracusan coins, shows three running legs like spokes of a wheel, with wings on their ankles and a Gorgon's head as a hub. But at the southeast cape, the land slopes rather gently to the sea. The axis of history runs between Aetna and Eryx. Mount Eryx and the table-land of Enna in the center of the island were shrines; Mount Aetna, a burial mound. Hesiod's *Theogony* describes their related origin.

When the world was young, Heaven and Earth—Ouranos and Gea—begot and birthed twelve titans. The last-born, Kronos, with the connivance of his mother, emasculated his father with a sickle. Afterwards, he dropped the sickle. It fell on Sicily. In classical Greek, the word for sickle is *drepana*. The hook of land at the northwest corner of the island is still called Trapani.

Where Heaven's severed genitals fell into the sea, the love-goddess, Aphrodite, rose full-blown, her chariot a cockle-shell. Above Trapani, she made the sheer, pine-sheathed point that overlooks island and ocean her favorite shrine; among the ruins of successive centuries, stones of its ancient altar are still distinguishable.

The height was named Mount Eryx in memory of a giant who was her son. Herakles, visiting Sicily on his way home from his labor of recovering Geryon's stolen cattle in Spain, playfully undertook to wrestle with the local giants. Eryx expired in his too-powerful clinch. Abashed and regretful, Herakles ordered the aborigines to give Eryx a fine funeral. Medieval Sicilian peasants who broke into a cave at the foot of Mount Eryx stared aghast at sight of a colossal male skeleton.

Earth mated not only with Heaven, but with Chaos. This union produced the monster Typhoes. Fire ran in its veins, blazed red from the eyes of its hundred black-snake heads. It had been prophesied that like father like son, the last-born of Kronos would kill his sire and reign in his stead, and so it happened. That was how Zeus became lord of all the Olympians. He also slaughtered Typhoes. For a weapon, he used an instrument invented by the Cyclops and adopted by three mighty brothers in three different forms: Poseidon wielded a trident, Hades a pitchfork, Zeus a three-pronged thunderbolt.

The Power of Typhoes

With sizzling thrusts, he struck each of Typhoes' hissing heads separately. But the limp, fiery mass continued to writhe. Zeus thrust it deep into the soil of northeast Sicily, piled earth upon it in a stupendous cone.

Beneath the peak called Aetna the fire and the twitching did not cease. From the south central part of Sicily up the mainland beyond Naples sulphurous fumes and steaming water spouted from crevices and surged in caves. Not only at Aetna but across the Straits of Messina, up the peninsula to Vesuvius and beyond,

burning lava spilled over the surface from scores of cones. Early Greek sailors named the area above the Bay of Naples the Phlegraean (Flaming) Fields.

As to Aetna itself, Vergil's *Aeneid* describes how

Ever and anon it discharges at heaven a mirky cloud,
A swirl of pitch-black smoke lurid with white-hot cinders,
And volleys huge balls of flame, singeing the very stars.
Ever and anon, as if the mountain's guts were being coughed up,
It belches rock, and groaning, vomits out thick streams
Of lava, seething up from its roots.

Hades, the king of the underworld, became worried lest this rock-lifting turbulence open courses of light into his dim kingdom of the dead. In his black-horsed chariot, he set out for Sicily.

Idling on Eryx, Aphrodite observed his approach. Mischiefminded, she signed to her attendant Eros to loose a shaft from his little quiver. He bent his bow. The arrow struck.

Hades was just approaching the great central table-land called Enna, Demeter's favorite seat. Along the leafy shore of nearby Lake Pergusa, Demeter's daughter Persephone was playing with the wood-nymphs. Looking down from his chariot, the smitten Hades sighted her.

Quickly, he dismounted, seized and raped her; then, opening the waters of the lake with his pitchfork, he snatched her away.

The nymph Cyane saw all, and told. Hades turned her into the eastern river that enters the sea near Syracuse.

At Enna, distraught Demeter sorrowed on the black crag where the stone steps of her temple now lead blindly up to nothingness—long ago, the rock shelf called Demeter's Balcony splintered and fell away. With torches lit at Aetna she searched for her daughter across starving and desolate fields where no harvests 25 grew. In all the lands of Greece, the sterile earth suffered with her; only when Zeus forced Hades to yield Persephone for two-thirds of each year was Demeter content that during those months the earth should bear again.

These ancient myths were awesomely believable when I stood near the tomb of Typhoes on a wild day in early March. A battered bus had left Catania at six-thirty in the morning, its passengers mostly maintenance men for the road. Looping his way with periodic halts, often in low gear and for the last few kilometers with icy caution, at a turn-out a mile and a quarter above sea-level, the driver swung round and cut his motor. We were near the terminus of the cable-car that in summer dangles its suspended way another half-mile up to the observatory near the rim of the volcano. A thinly-clad man from Lyon and I were the remaining passengers.

"At half-past four this afternoon," the conductor announced as he prepared to close up the vehicle, "the bus goes back." No, nothing sooner.

Appalled, the thinly-clad man hastened to the staffed but otherwise empty hostel beside the terminus, to shiver out the eight hours before its tiny fire. The knowing ones—the men from the bus and the boy at the coffee-machine—estimated the wind velocity at sixty-five.

From time to time I came in for hot coffee and a memorable lunch, but through the day, jack-knifed against the gusts, I made forays to the lea of the terminus building. Back to the wall, under shelter of its overhanging eaves, I watched the weather blow by in a repeated spectrum: gold to purple; sun to snow; rain to darkness; sun again; successions of blinding light and lowering shadow.

In clear intervals, up the mountain from the drifted foreground, 26 I could see white-mounded shoulder leading to white-mounded shoulder until the last profiled curvature continued in piled white cloud, distinguishable from the snow only because of its massive motion.

Suddenly, the motion enveloped the sun. A curtain of great white flakes dropped from the eaves, isolating me on my narrow ledge.

When the flurry slackened, a subsidiary cone below me to the east had become a huge white china bowl, partly filled with soft snow. Then the blizzard turned to heavy rain; in no time, the bowl became an enormous black cauldron, empty and hard.

Beyond the edge of the road, fringed with ice-stiffened, wind-bent grasses, the mountain drops off sharply. Far down, the great Catanian plain stretched away southward, rimmed on the east by the sea, its spring greens splotched here and there with moving purple of cloud shadows. Over the workers in those fields, the clouds whose mist wet my face would drift a mile high.

Seeing, I believed that beneath his funeral mound, Typhoes dominates the western side of the Italian boot and a full two-thirds of Sicily.

On a train journey in southern Sicily, from Gela around to Syracuse, an oil geologist, elated into generosity by having that day selected the site for his first big drill, let me pore over his portfolio of detailed maps.

As I opened it, I asked him a question whose answer taught me a new word. In the center of the island I had noticed a curious formation riding the crest of a long ridge: an enormous vertical-sided rock, unmistakably unrelated to the rest of the landscape. How had it got there? He explained that at one time older mountains in south Sicily were sinking while newer ones in the north were thrusting up, brittle and tall. Pieces broke off; some, bouncing, landed on the sinking ridges. Very recently, oil geologists have named such a fragment 'olisthostroma,' from the Greek words for 'slip' and 'cover.' Colonists were delighted when they came upon such a formation: it provided a high rock for their citadel.

Then we bent over the maps. In the southeast, put a pin between Ragusa and Modica: the eighteenth century baroque portals of their churches decorate towns wholly rebuilt after the earthquake of 1693. At the Straits, put another pin between Messina and Reggio di Calabria, where 84,000 people died in twenty shaken minutes in the earthquake of 1908. Among the Lipari isles slightly northwest, put a pin between now-quiescent Vulcan, whose rifts still exhale smoke and bubbling hot springs that permit year-round sea bathing, and active and thoughtfully smoking Stromboli; their destructiveness has always been confined by the surrounding sea. On the Italian peninsula, put a pin between Pompeii and Herculaneum, where fall-out of pumice particles and white-hot ash blown skyward by Vesuvius buried towns and

people in 79 A.D. Put a last pin between Naples and Cumae where hot springs, live steam, sulphur vapors and thirteen now-extinct cones substantiate early Greek travellers' tales of fields that glowed as the fresh outpourings of Aetna glow in the half-light of pre-dawn or dusk today.

The line of pins is the major geologic fault-line of a land-mass that was once continuous; only last century it was known as the Kingdom of the Two Sicilies.

There are many minor fault-lines—in northwest Sicily, the geologist and I had each visited Segesta, I to observe the temple, he to examine the fault-line in its background hill. On the south coast, the colossal shatterings that took down Akragas and Selinus must have been even more awesome than the earthquake that strewed on the ground the columns of Zeus's sanctuary at Olympia in Greece.

The Power of Typhoes

Pindar, in his First Pythian ode, describes this landscape in the language of myth:

. . . he who sprawls, God's enemy, in the pit of Tartaros,
Typhon, the hundred-headed, whom of old
the cave of many names in Kilikia bred; and now
the sea-dykes above Kymai are set over him;
Sicily crushes his shaggy
chest; the sky's pillar is piled above him,
Aitna of the snows, year-long
minister of the cleaving ice.

Thence erupt pure founts of unapproachable fire
from the secret places within; by day the rivers spout in a flood of
*   smoke,*
shot through with shining; by dark from the rock
the red flame rolling plunges to the deep sea-plain in tumult.
The monster hurls aloft such spouts
of weird flame; a portent and a wonder to behold, a wonder even to
*   hear from those who have seen.*
Thus, beneath the pinnacles dark in leaves of Aitna he lies shackled
underground, and the jagged bed rips all his back that is cramped
*   against it.*

Such stirrings of Typhoes have been disasters. Yet the lava lipping over Aetna's rim is a source and symbol of life as well as death in Sicily. The paradox revealed itself below snow-line as my bus descended. It is easy to see where successive lava streams, old and recent, have spilled down the mountain, some of them all the way to the sea. Once they were hot and malleable; today they are cold and hard.

Below the snow, the highest black landscapes are of an unearthly desolation. On this moon-surface, no spring comes; not even a lizard moves. Aetna's characteristic creatures are the enormous winged black beetles with which Aristophanes, in his satire *Peace*, replaced the winged white horse, Pegasus.

The ground is as dark as the mourning clothes which Sicilian peasant women put on when hardly more than brides and wear until a little strip of black cloth is tacked to the front door in witness of their own passing, dangling there until weathered duncolor by the sun. In these fields are quarried the bands of black stone that decorate church portals, framing the Friday night of an unresurrected crucifixion, their little human counterparts the black-bordered notices pasted on village walls by relatives of a deceased.

Yet in the life of a mountain, a century is a moment; when mellowed and decomposed by sun, wind and rain, lava becomes the richest of fruit-bearing soil. Even as I rode, a sudden rainbow, arcing out of black desolation, lifted a promise of fertility.

The blood oranges of Sicily are rooted in once-volcanic rock. Farmers mine the aging lava, and mulch the crumbling stone into the wholly-matured black soil of their vineyards. With spring, the black vines, pruned in February till they stand like knotted clouts of tarred rope, leaf into pale green overnight, and weigh their wires with autumn abundance.

The Power of Typhoes

The Roman historian, Strabo, speaks of similar yields below Vesuvius:

"Perhaps, too, this is the cause of the fruitfulness of the country all round the mountain; just as at Catana, it is said, that part of the country which had been covered with ash-dust from the hot

ashes carried up into the air by the fire of Aetna made the land suited to the vine; for it contains the substance that fattens both the soil which is burnt out and that which produces the fruits."

As if a huge floral wreath were flung in festival over the cone of Aetna, a ring of citrus orchards circles its lower slopes. On their trees, ripe fruit still hangs when bees are summoned by the fragrance of new bloom. From Catania, the little narrow-gauge cars of the CircumAetnaea Railway trace the wreath around the mountain, stopping at Paterno, Adrano, Brontë (the name-giving town of the duchy bestowed on Lord Nelson in gratitude for his protection of the island from Napoleon) and Randazzo, and thence down to the sea again at Riposto.

At this level, Zeus is believably master of Typhoes. The mountain of mountains is at least to be looked at with the loving vigilance that is in the eyes of a Greek sailor when he looks at the sea. I did not forget the blind and wilful power whose force had   33 beat upon me above snow-line, but here I saw Aetna in beneficent and mellow mood.

Above Randazzo, at sunset in clear weather, the snowfields turn to rose; the black rim of the crater's edge where no snow can linger looks very narrow; the ever-present wisp of condensed steam rising from its center drifts off another way.

At Reggio di Calabria across the Straits, before the morning mist over the water is sucked back into the sea, the high massif is as much a part of Italy as Sicily.

When I stood on Demeter's steps at Enna, the white height lifted serene above and beyond the tumult of a raging valley storm.

From Taormina, the panorama of mountain, fruited peninsula and many harbored coast was a mirage of plenty—and so it must have been described by voyaging Greek sailors when they returned to city states where colonies were formed.

CHAPTER II

Land of Epic Heroes

If a first legendary overlay of the map of Magna Graecia locates the preferred sites of the Olympians, a second marks the scenes and settlements through which Minoan and Mycenaean myths unite the western with the central and eastern shores of the Mediterranean.

It was to Magna Graecia that the master-craftsman, Daedalus, air-borne on the first man-made wings, escaped from the wrath of King Minos of Crete. This artificer was as wily with devices as Odysseus was with words. Repeatedly, he invited the royal anger. Repeatedly, he invented his way out of its consequences.

The first incident occurred when he fashioned the wooden cow that permitted Minos' wife Pasiphae to consort with Poseidon's great white bull and conceive the bull-headed man, the Minotaur. The humiliated king turned on the craftsman, but Daedalus mollified his master by devising a labyrinth to confine the monster and keep it out of sight.

Next, the king's daughter Ariadne fell in love with Theseus when that prince arrived from Athens as one of the youths and maidens delivered in annual tribute to be fed to the Minotaur. Daedalus, himself an Athenian by birth, gave the princess a thread by which Theseus could find his way out of the labyrinth. The prince killed the monster, thereby relieving his city of further tribute, and took Ariadne with him when he sailed away.

This time, Minos condemned Daedalus to death, and his son Icarus along with him. Quickly, Daedalus contrived wings; the gaping Cretans saw the pair rise aloft and soar away.

Icarus died a cautionary death. Stunting high and wide, he flew too close to the sun; the heat melted the wax that attached his wings. His body plummeted into the sea. But Daedalus landed safely.

Legends vary as to where he alighted. One tale has him touch down on the south-central shore of Sicily, in the region of Agrigento, and there enter the service of King Kokalos. His first ingratiating enterprise was to erect an impregnable new citadel at a site called Kamikos—perhaps the present Sant' Angelo Muxaro, where a number of Mycenaean tombs have been found. Then he channeled nearby hot springs to provide imposing baths. The historian Diodorus Siculus, who describes many of Daedalus' feats, tells of a grotto "where he so successfully expelled the steam caused by the fire which burned in it that those who frequented the grotto got into a perspiration imperceptibly because of the gentle action of the heat, and gradually, and actually with pleasure to themselves, they cured the infirmities of their bodies without experiencing any annoyance from the heat."

At the temple of Aphrodite on Eryx, Daedalus seems to have experimented with cantilever construction: "he constructed a wall upon the very crag, by this means extending in an astonishing manner the overhanging ledge of the crag." To adorn this temple, the craftsman fashioned a golden model of Aphrodite's animal, "making it the perfect image of an actual ram."

Word of Daedalus' exploits spread over the water. When King Minos learned of his whereabouts, he readied a huge fleet and himself led the pursuit. He established a beachhead at the place still known as Heraklea Minoa, and demanded return of Daedalus.

King Kokalos, wily as his artificer, invited Minos to Kamikos for lavish entertainment, steamed him to death at the baths, gave him a splendid funeral at the beachhead with burial in "a tomb of two storeys, in the part of it which was hidden underground they placed the bones, and in that which lay open to gaze they made a shrine to Aphrodite."

Sir Arthur Evans uncovered such a shrine-tomb at the Minoan palace of Knossos in Crete. In historic times, when Theron was tyrant of Akragas, Minos's remains are reported to have been ceremonially returned to Crete.

Evidence of settlement at Heracleia Minoa and Cattolica Minoa has recently been recovered, part of it on the very verge of the sea, part of it further inland. The land along this coast rises in high sandy dunes that drop off sheer to a fairly broad beach. Along their crest, a fourth century B.C. wall has been unearthed, and at one end of it the well-fitted stones of a small circular building, perhaps a council house. Further inland are the remains of a theater.

The Latin *Aeneid* and the Greek *Odyssey* both people Magna Graecia for the contests between the holders of the eastern and the holders of the western coasts of Sicily, and between the Greeks in Sicily and Southern Italy and the rising power of Rome.

Persistent legend as well as epic credits Trojan refugees with
plantation of colonies in northwest Sicily from Trapani to Segesta,

numbering Aeneas' half-brother, king of Phrygia, as well as Aeneas among the founders. The *Aeneid* takes its hero around the island, from the storm that threw him onto its east coast to his landing at Trapani, thence to North Africa, back to Trapani, and finally to Italy, his victories in Campania and his triumphal fulfilment of his destiny as founder of Rome.

This epic was written at the end of the first century B.C.; its geography was accurately familiar to its author. When the *Odyssey* was composed, by contrast, the western Mediterranean world was legendary country of vague outline, inhabited by curious and often terrible sorcerers and monsters. Odysseus was a wanderer among them: the scenes of many of his encounters have baffled scholars over the centuries. Yet his storm-battered voyaging in western waters indubitably took him from island to mainland to island, back and forth over the entire region that was subsequently Greek, and exact location is occasionally possible.

Both heroes met danger at the base of Aetna from the Cyclops whose red-glowing single eyes resembled the subsidiary cones of the great mountain. Odysseus' adventure among these cannibalistic giants provides not only one of the most vivid episodes in the *Odyssey* but the action of the only complete surviving example of the satyr-play that conventionally followed a presentation of tragic drama, Euripides' *Cyclops*.

Landing on the coast below Aetna with twelve of his men, Odysseus was trapped by Polyphemus, who penned them in a great cave along with his flock and began to eat them singly at his leisure.

The wily Greek plied the giant with drink, then blinded his single eye with a log heated to burning point in the fire over which the Cyclops was roasting his companions. Thereafter, the survivors escaped from the cave by clinging to the underbellies of 39 the sheep when the sightless shepherd let them out to pasture. Odysseus describes the end of the adventure:

> . . . . *I took*
> *The woolliest ram, the choicest of the flock,*
> *and hung myself under his kinky belly,*
> *pulled up tight, with fingers twisted deep*
> *in sheepskin ringlets for an iron grip . . . .*
> *Blinded, and sick with pain from his head wound,*
> *the master stroked each ram, then let it pass,*
> *but my men riding on the pectoral fleece*
> *the giant's blind hands blundering never found.*

When they regained their ship, Odysseus, heady with victory, could not refrain from yelling a parting taunt across the water. Infuriated, Polyphemus broke off a crag and pelted the direction of the sound. Today, at Acitrezza, visitors are shown the Cyclopean Rocks, scattered out from shore where they very nearly achieved Polyphemus' purpose:

> *The blind thing in his doubled fury broke*
> *A hilltop in his hands and heaved it after us.*
> *Ahead of our black prow it struck and sank*
> *whelmed in a spuming geyser, a giant wave*
> *that washed the ship stern foremost back to shore.*
> *I got the longest boathook out and stood*
> *fending us off, with furious nods to all*
> *to put their backs into a racing stroke—*
> *row, row, or perish.*

In the rush to get away, one hapless crewman, Achemenides, was left behind. Aeneas and his Trojans picked him up, close to starvation, three months later, when a violent storm in the Straits

40

of Messina drove them too into the Cyclops' harbor. Vergil tells
how, in departing, they glimpsed the giant:

. . . . . we saw that same shepherd, that Polyphemus—
A monster, grisly, misshapen, titanic, his eye gone.
He carries the trunk of a pine tree to guide and support him walking:
The fleecy sheep go with him—they are his only pleasure
And consolation in woe.
When he had come to the sea's edge and touched the surging deep,
He washed the socket of his eye, which oozed blood, with sea-water,
Gritting his teeth and groaning; then waded into the deep sea,
Yet even there the water did not come up to his waist.
Frightened, we hurried to get far away, taking on board
That Greek who so merited mercy, and stealthily cutting the cables:
Frantically we tugged at the oars, we swept the sea's face.
He sensed us, veered his steps toward the noise of our passage.
But when he found there was no way of laying his hands upon us
And he was falling behind in the race with the waves which carried us,
Then he let out a stupendous bellow, shivering the whole
Expanse of the sea, shaking Italy to its core
With fright, and reverberating through Aetna's anfractuous caves.

Once away, Aeneas set a southward course, heeding a warning
not to try the perilous passage where the twin dangers of Scylla
and Charybdis flanked the narrow straits between Sicily and Italy:

Once on a time, they say, these two lands were a single
Country; then there came a convulsion of nature which tore them
Hugely asunder—the ages can bring such immense geological
Change—and the sea rushed violently in between them, dividing
Italy from Sicily, severing their coasts and washing
Cities and fields on either side with a narrow strait.
Scylla guards the right shore, insatiable Charybdis

The left . . . . It's advisable
To fetch a long compass, although it protracts the voyage, and sail
Right round the Sicilian cape of Pachynum, a southernmost mark,
Rather than to set eyes on that freakish Scylla within
Her cavern vast or the rocks where her sea-blue hounds are baying.

Aeneas, in any case a man of caution, could take the long view, for he was westbound, trying to reach Rome. Odysseus, by contrast, battered, shipwrecked, driven from one western coast to another, and by no means a patient man, was eastbound. Though thwarted for two decades, his objective remained his island kingdom of Ithaca in the Ionian sea between Greece and Sicily.

Therefore, though warned by a precise description of the perils of the passage, he decided to attempt the straits when the sorceress Circe finally let him leave her west Italian shore. She said:

. . . . . A second course
lies between headlands. One is a sharp mountain . . . .
No mortal man could scale it, nor so much
as land there, not with twenty hands and feet,
so sheer the cliffs are—as of polished stone.
Midway that height, a cavern full of mist
opens toward Erebos and evening. Skirting
this in the lugger, great Odysseus,
your master bowman, shooting from the deck,
would come short of the cavemouth with his shaft;
but that is the den of Skylla, where she yaps
abominably, a newborn whelp's cry,
though she is huge and monstrous. God or man,
no one could look on her in joy. Her legs—
and there are twelve—are like great tentacles,
unjointed, and upon her serpent necks
are borne six heads like nightmares of ferocity,

with triple serried rows of fangs and deep
gullets of black death. Half her length, she sways
her heads on air, outside her horrid cleft,
hunting the sea around that promontory
for dolphins, dogfish, or what bigger game
thundering Amphitritê feeds in thousands.
And no ship's company can claim
to have passed her without loss and grief; she takes
from every ship, one man for every gullet.
The opposite point seems more a tongue of land
you'd touch with a good bowshot, at the narrows.
A great wild fig, a shaggy mass of leaves,
grows on it, and Kharybdis lurks below
to swallow down the dark sea tide. Three times
from dawn to dusk she spews it up
and sucks it down again three times, a whirling
maelstrom; if you come upon her then
The god who makes earth tremble could not save you.
No, hug the cliff of Skylla, take your ship
Through on a racing stroke. Better to mourn
six men than lose them all, and the ship, too.

The hero lost his six men, passed the narrows, landed safely on Sicily. The strain over, he fell asleep, content to be eastbound again.

But close to their camp, his men saw grazing the cattle of the sun god Helios. It was sacrilege to touch them, and they very well knew it. Yet Odysseus awoke to the smell of barbecue.

Helios complained to Zeus. When Odysseus sailed, the avenging Olympian

. . . . piled a thunderhead
above the ship, while gloom spread on the ocean.

43

We held our course, but briefly. Then the squall
struck whining from the west, with gale force . . . . . .
. . . . on the after deck
The mast had hit the steersman a slant blow
bashing the skull in, knocking him overside. . . .

A direct lightning stroke upended the ship, spilling all over-board. Every one except Odysseus drowned. He managed to straddle the empty keel but could not steer. Inexorably, the wind drove him back to the Straits.

There, as the whirlpool drank the tide, a billow
tossed me, and I sprang for the great fig tree,
catching on like a bat under a bough.

He clung there until the fragments of the ship came back up from the whirlpool at twilight. Then,

. . . . . I let go with hands and feet, plunging
straight into the foam between the timbers,
pulled astride, and rowed hard with my hands
to pass by Skylla.

Back in Tyrrhenian waters, after nine days of drifting he washed up on Kalypso's isle, further than ever from his destination.

Though the Trojans avoided the perils of the Straits, Aeneas, even as Odysseus, continued to be thwarted of his destiny. In the course of their circumnavigation of the island, his aged father died at Trapani. Since Aphrodite had been his immortal consort, Aeneas buried him close to her shrine.

Once more they took ship and set a northward course, but the 45 wrath of Hera, unreconstructed partisan of Greek against Trojan in the great war, intervened. Forced to turn and run before a violent wind, Aeneas' fleet was blown to Africa. The ships made land at the recently founded Phoenician colony of Carthage. Its ruler was Tyrian Dido.

Lest Dido's soldiers attack the Trojans, Aphrodite inflamed the queen with a consuming passion for Aeneas. Responding, he dallied so long that Zeus was forced to send a messenger to remind him of his mission.

The arriving envoy

> . . . . . . *noticed Aeneas superintending the work on towers*
> *And new buildings: he wore a sword studded with yellow*
> *Jaspers, and a fine cloak of glowing Tyrian purple*
> *Hung from his shoulders—the wealthy Dido had fashioned it,*
> *Interweaving the fabric with threads of gold, as a present for him.*
> *Mercury went for him at once:—So now you are laying*
> *Foundations for lofty Carthage, building a beautiful city*
> *To please a woman, lost to the interests of your own realm?*

Thus rebuked, Aeneas departed.

The rejected Dido killed herself, but not before she had laid a Carthaginian curse on Aeneas and his Roman descendants to the last generation:

> *Let you, my Tyrians, sharpen your hatred upon his children*
> *And all their seed for ever: send this as a present to*
> *My ghost. Between my people and his, no love, no alliance!*
> *Rise up from my dead bones, avenger! Rise up, one*
> *To hound the Trojan settlers with fire and steel remorselessly,*
> *Now, some day, whenever the strength for it shall be granted!*
> *Shore to shore, sea to sea, weapon to weapon opposed—*
> *I call down a feud between them and us to the last generation!*

Aeneas returned to Trapani, held funeral games there in honor of his father, and left behind a colony when a fair wind finally took his expedition to Italy. Northwest of Naples,

. . . . at long last they slid to the shores of Euboean Cumae.
The bows are swung round to face the sea, the vessels made fast with
The biting hook of their anchors, and the sheer sterns are lining
The beach . . . . .

In all versions of the story of Daedalus, Apollo's temple at Cumae, with its celebrated carved doors, were his work; in Vergil's description of his flight from Crete, Cumae becomes also his first landing place:

Here he first came to earth, hung up his apparatus
Of flight as a thanks-offering to Phoebus, and built a great temple.
On its door was depicted the death of Androgeos; also the legend
Of how the Athenians, poor souls, were forced to pay yearly tribute
With seven of their sons—the scene when the lots had just been drawn.
Facing this, there's a bas-relief; with Crete rising out of the waves;
Pasiphae, cruelly fated to lust after a bull,
And privily covered; the hybrid fruit of that monstrous union—
The Minotaur, a memento of her unnatural love:
Here's the insoluble maze constructed by Daedalus;
Yet, sympathising with Ariadne in her great passion,
He gives her himself the clue to the maze's deceptive windings,
And guides with a thread the blind steps of Theseus. In the artifact
Icarus too would have had a prominent place, if his father's
Grief had allowed: but twice, trying to work the boy's fall
In gold, did Daedalus' hands fail him . . . .

From the Cumaean Sibyl, Aeneas heard again, along with prophecy of trials ahead, a confirmation of his destiny. 47

There's a huge cave hollowed out from the flank of Cumae's hill;
A hundred wide approaches it has, a hundred mouths
From which there issue a hundred voices, the Sibyl's answers.
They had reached its threshold when 'Time it is to ask your destiny'
The Sibyl cried, 'for lo! the god is with me.' And speaking,
There by the threshold, her features, her colour were all at once
Different, her hair flew wildly about; her breast was heaving,
Her fey heart swelled in ecstasy; larger than life she seemed,
More than mortal her utterance . . . .

With her as guide, before proceeding northward, Aeneas entered the kingdom of the dead to consult the shade of his father. Nearby Lake Avernus permitted an easy descent; Strabo said of it, "these hill-brows, because of the superstition of man, used to make the gulf a shadowy place. And the natives used to add the further fable that all birds that fly over it fall down into the water, being killed by the vapours that rise from it." The word Avernus means birdless.

Re-emerging into the world of light, Aeneas approached the definitive single combat in which he defeated Turnus, King of Italy.

Thereafter, the legendary Trojan losers became the historic Roman winners. Beginning in the third century B.C., they enveloped first the western colonies of Greece, then the Greek peninsula, the islands, the Hellenized Near East, till all were gathered into one vast imperium.

CHAPTER III

When the Greeks Came

Ending as it does with the location of historic peoples and persons, the legendary overlay of the map of Magna Graecia foreshadows a third series of identifications, placing the tribes and civilizations that were there when the Greeks came. For though among the early Greeks the very remoteness of Sicily and Italy encouraged myth and epic, the unknown spaces of subsequent Greek colonization were in fact not empty.

On the Greek peninsula, the incoming tides of Greek migration overwhelmed the paleolithic aborigines, whether shapers and movers of the huge-stoned Pelasgian walls that the Greeks attributed to the Cyclops or shy Shore People living in wattled huts.   *49*

Greece became all Greek, though divided into city-states that warred almost unceasingly with one another.

But Sicily and Italy, until incorporated into the Roman imperium, never became all anything; quarrels among the Greeks were complicated by clashes with settlements of other cultures. Along the Italian boot, the Greek coastal cities were overlooked by powerful tribes entrenched in the lowering hills. In Sicily, Greek settlers might dominate the eastern end of the island, but the northwestern end was dominated by Punic settlers, and many aboriginal fastnesses, Hellenized but of uncertain loyalty, stood in between.

Little enough is known about the earlier peoples of Sicily, yet though they were driven from the coasts to the interior by the coming of the Greeks and the Phoenicians, their consequential settlements remained factors in subsequent balances of power, whether as allies or enemies, mercenaries or serfs, or briefly successful irredentists in the fifth century under their military leader, Ducetius.

Stone age remains, from paleolithic to neolithic, are numerous in many parts of the island and in some of the surrounding smaller island groups. Cave dwellers in Levanzo and Favignana, two of the Egadi Islands off the tip of the northwest coast, have left designs of men and of animals, some incised and some painted, on cavern walls. On Monte Pellegrino, just outside Palermo, the figures in the paintings are among the earliest representations of the human form.

The volcanic Lipari islands, a good two hours' sail by competent steamer northwest from the Sicilian port of Milazzo, were the legendary home of the windmaster King Aeolus. Polybius' account of the climate on Vulcan substantiates the legend:

When the south wind is going to blow, a thick haze gathers all round the island so that not even Sicily is visible; but when the north wind is going to blow clear flames spring up to some height from the crater I was speaking of and louder rumblings than usual issue from it. The signs foretelling a west wind are halfway between the two . . . . from the difference of the rumblings, and from the direction from which the discharges and the smoke and flame come, one can foretell from what quarter the wind will blow even three days later . . . . So that what seems to us Homer's most mythical statement, when he calls Aeolus the dispenser of the winds, was not quite an idle tale, but darkly hinted at the truth.

In their slender boats, the Lipari islanders carried on commerce over much of the Mediterranean. The staple of their exchanges was obsidian. This very hard, glass-like substance, formed in the course of volcanic eruption, can be sharpened to points and edges even finer than those of flint. Before metals were known, the ancient world prized it above all other materials for weapons, tools, occasional art objects. Literally living on volcanos, the Lipari islanders were in an economic position comparable to today's dealers in industrial diamonds.

As seamen, they must have been spectacular. Enumerating their votives at Delphi, Pausanias notes:

> . . . the Liparaeans were bidden by the Pythian priestess to fight the Tyrrhenians with the fewest possible ships. So they put to sea with five galleys to meet the Tyrrhenians. The latter thinking it shame if they were not a match for the Liparaeans at sea, put out to meet them with the same number of ships. So the Liparaeans captured these ships, and when another five afterwards put to sea against them, they captured them too, and they conquered a third, and likewise a fourth squadron of five ships each. Therefore they dedicated at Delphi as many images of Apollo as they had captured ships.

51

When the Greeks Came

Down the centuries, all occupants of Lipari have used the rock known as the Castello for their major citadel. Their records, deposited in vertical layers, therefore provide the kind of chronological sequence that rejoicing archaeologists refer to as a 'tell.'

On this rock, outside the Renaissance building now used as a museum, clustered oval outlines of Bronze Age huts have been uncovered; inside, displays include incised and painted pottery of a wide range of dates, shapes and colors, delicate faience beads, and objects which document the islanders' exchange with Mycenaean centers. In the garden, high above sea and plain and surrounded by softly fronding pepper trees, is a collection of large rectangular stone coffins with fitted lids, many wine-red in color.

On Sicily itself, the stone-age necropolis slightly inland from Syracuse at Pantalica is perhaps the most spectacular of pre-Greek centers. Rock tombs there are numbered by thousands, and cover a time-span from the thirteenth to the eighth century B.C.

Located as close to each other as headstones in a cemetery are chambers, sometimes with inner benches, cut into the steep limestone cliffs near the top of a high plateau isolated by the deep canyons of two rivers. The sheer sides of the surrounding valleys are cultivated in narrow terraces; backlit by morning sun, the green of their spring wheat seems to fall in cascades from ledge to ledge.

Many of the grave goods found in this necropolis are in the Syracuse Museum, together with finds from other southeastern sites, including Castelluccio. The portal stones that closed tomb entrances there are striking examples of aboriginal stone-carving. 53

These stone-age peoples worshipped a fertility goddess, Hybla, akin to Demeter. Their god of Aetna, Hadranus, had for sons the mysterious Palici; of the geysers at their shrine, Diodorus Siculus writes:

> For first of all there are craters which are not at all large in size, but they throw up extraordinary streams of water from a depth beyond telling and have very much the nature of cauldrons which are heated by a strong fire and throw up boiling water. Now the water that is thrown up gives the impression of being boiling hot, but this is not known for certain because of the fact that no man dares touch it; for the amazement caused by the spout of water is so great that men believe the phenomenon to be due to some divine power. For not only does the water give out a strongly sulphurous smell but the yawning mouth emits a mighty and terrifying roar; and what is still more astonishing than this, the water neither pours over nor recedes, but has a motion and force in its current that lifts it to a marvelous height. Since so divine a majesty pervades the sacred area, the most sacred oaths are taken there and men who swear falsely are immediately overtaken by the punishment of heaven; thus certain men have lost their sight when they depart from the sacred precinct.

The Sikels from whom the island took its name were only one of three separate groups of aborigines to survive into historic times in numbers sufficient to make themselves felt. Settled in the east of Sicily, they are believed to have come from Italy, and to have had a King, Italus, who gave his name to the peninsula.

Except in emphasizing that they were a separate people, ancient writers disagreed about the origins of the Sikans who inhabited the center of the island, some saying that they were Sicilian aborigines, others that they came from Spain by way of Italy, still others that they were an Italian people who preceded the Sikels from Italy. Diodorus believed that they had originally settled in the eastern part of the island, but had withdrawn westward because of frequent lava-flow from eruptions of Aetna.

The Elymians, who lived in the northwest where legend ascribes colonies to Troy and other Asia Minor cities, are perhaps the most shadowy of all, but excavations in the early 1960's produced initial evidence of their language: pottery shards were found inscribed in Greek characters but in a language that is not Greek.

By the eighth century, these early peoples were caught in a pincers of simultaneous new settlement. Whether or not urged on by the curse of Dido, Carthaginian invasion and colonization enveloped the sites of legendary Trojan settlements, forming a continuous crescent from Lilybaeum (Marsala) in the west around to Panormus (Palermo) in the north. Only sixty sea miles separate Carthage and Trapani; from Sicilian Mount Eryx on a clear day one can see North African Cap Bon.

The island of Motya in Marsala's protected harbor afforded exactly the kind of geographic location that Phoenicians most prized. Tyre, chief among their Asia Minor cities of origin, was at this period an offshore island separated from the mainland by narrow straits—man-made causeways such as that constructed by the conquering Alexander the Great and natural fill had not yet closed them up. This combination of access and protection so suited the purposes of venturesome, trading seafarers that their offshoots and descendants sought similar terrain when colonizing the shores of Africa and the Western Mediterranean. At Carthage, at Mogador on the West African coast, at Gades (Cadiz) in Spain and in the bay of Marsala in Sicily, they found what they were

56 looking for.

Punic power in Sicily centered in Motya on the west coast just as Greek power centered in Syracuse on the east coast. Over the centuries, the line of demarcation between Greek and Punic spheres of influence was pushed east or west as one power-complex or the other amassed supplies, secured allies, developed able generals.

The island of Motya is privately owned, so permission to visit must be obtained in advance. It is currently under extensive excavation. Though affected by the general subsidence of the Mediterranean shoreline—the stone-paved causeway at the northern edge of the island, connecting it with the mainland, is now slightly under water—the remains of the early historic period have happily been relatively little overlaid by subsequent building.

The construction being revealed includes an example of the distinctive and characteristic Punic harbors called cothons. These were very shallow rectangular or circular basins, paved wet docks with access to deep water through guarded channels, capable of accommodating considerable numbers of vessels in maximum safety. The cothons at Carthage, during the Punic wars, are said to have held over two hundred ships.

The small size of the Motya cothon may be accounted for by the fact that the island is protected to the north and west by a dogleg of land formed by the larger Isola Grande; the waters of the surrounding lagoon are therefore quiet enough for reliable anchorage.

On the lower part of the Italian peninsula, the Greek settlements, in their shallow coastal enclaves, faced opposition at least as difficult as that of their counterparts in Sicily. At their backs were stout tribesmen fighting from the inhospitable hills—Messapians, Brutii, Lucanians, Samnites—ruder than the Sicilian aborigines, rarely Hellenized, repeatedly successful as conquerors. 57

When the Greeks Came

Further north, the Greek line had to be held against a highly civilized power. Above the Tiber, in cities that like the Greek cities were located close to the coast, the cultivated and mysterious Etruscans, perhaps themselves arrivals from the Eastern Mediterranean, flourished for a long interval and at the last supplied Rome with its pre-Republican Tarquin kings. Dionysus of Halicarnassus says of Etruscan Veii that it "was in no respect inferior to Rome as a place in which to live."

Until Rome expanded at the expense of both Greeks and Etruscans, the two engaged in much peaceful commerce interrupted by occasional battle. The Etruscans adopted the Greek alphabet to inscribe a language that is still as tantalizingly undeciphered as either the handful of comparably inscribed Elymian shards and Sikel inscriptions in Sicily or Linear A in Crete. Many of the most beautiful extant Greek vases, the earlier ones from Corinth and the Eastern Aegean, the later ones of Attic workmanship, are finds from Etruscan tombs—the superb collection of Greek imports and indigenous Etruscan terra cottas in the Villa Giulia in Rome and the Etruscan rooms in the National Museum in Palermo dramatize both the taste and the wealth of this elusive and attractive people.

Such were the communities that overlaid the map when, from the mid-eighth to the early sixth century B.C., one Greek colony after another arrived to rim the South Italian and Sicilian shores and, more sparsely, dot the French and Spanish coasts. Some came to escape persecution. More came to acquire wealth.

CHAPTER IV

Rush of Arrival

The great initiators of western colonization, founders of the first permanent settlements on both the Italian and the Sicilian coast, were Euboeians from the large island that is separated by narrow straits from the east coast of mainland Greece. Two of its cities, Chalcis and Eritrea, furnished a surprising succession of emigrants.

Their first Italian colony, the northern settlement that held the Greek line against Etruscan encroachment, was the earliest in all Magna Graecia: on the island of Ischia northwest of Naples, about 750 B.C., they planted Pithecusae. Their first Sicilian colony,   59

Naxos, arrived at Capo Schiso northeast of Mount Aetna some fifteen years later.

Within a generation, the settlers at Pithecusae abandoned their site in favor of a location on the opposite mainland shore, thenceforth known as Cumae (Kymai). Here they prospered so greatly that shortly they both took in adjacent territory and sent out settlers of their own. The colony itself first expanded southward, annexing the port of Dikearchia (Puteoli in St. Paul's time, Pozzuoli today.) Then, continuing south, it refounded the settlement of Parthenope in the Bay of Naples, calling it the New City, Neapolis.

These expansions were contiguous. But about 725 B.C. Eritreans and Cumaeans occupied the hook of land at the northeast tip of Sicily, where a nest of Cumaean pirates had informally preceded them. They called their city Zankle, the local Sikel word for sickle—for a time, the eastern as well as the western tip of the island was named for Kronos' instrument.

Zankle founded Mylae (Milazzo) along the north coast, and west of that, Himera; across the Strait, the city helped other Euboeians start Rhegium (Reggio di Calabria), bringing the sea passage between Sicily and Italy under united oversight.

These foundations were subsequently conquered by other Greeks, but for over three hundred years Cumae held its own.

Excavations at Pithecusae and Cumae have yielded two of the earliest Greek vases of the west. Both are exceptional in that they are inscribed. The skyphos (two-handled cup) from Pithecusae, to be seen at Lacco Ameno on Ischia, presents perhaps the earliest known alphabetic writing in Greek. Its owner, one Nestor, warns the unauthorized drinker: "He who drinks from Nestor's cup indeed drinks well, but the draught is a sudden aphrodisiac."

60   The inscription on the Protocorinthian araballos (scent con-

tainer) from Cumae carries a more childish threat, warning a potential thief that "I am Tataie's lekythos. May any one who steals me be struck blind."

It was at Cumae that the Romans coined a word for the Greeks. The peoples of the Greek peninsula had always referred to themselves as Hellenes; officially, the Greek nation styles itself the Kingdom of the Hellenes now. By a curious chance, its more usual designation originated in Italy.

The Cumaean settlers from Euboeia apparently had two groups of companions. If, in fact, citizens from Kyme in Asia Minor joined their band a clue is at hand as to the derivation of the colony's name. It seems more definite that in addition, there were neighbors from Boeotia; these were known as Graeoi because they worshipped an obscure goddess, Graea.

To the Romans, they were all Graeci—Greeks.

The area around Cumae—the ancient Flaming Fields and Lake Avernus—lends itself to mystery. Not only steam and gas but deposits of copper underlie the surface. The coming of the Bronze Age put a premium on this metal since bronze is made by combining copper and tin. The heavy-armored hoplite of classical times depended on it.

Of the miners of these seams, the Cimmerians, Strabo quotes the historian Ephorus as saying:

> They live in underground houses, which they call 'argillae', and it is through tunnels that they visit one another, back and forth, and also admit strangers to the oracle, which is situated far beneath the earth; and they live on what they get from mining, and from those who consult the oracle . . . and those who live about the oracle have an ancestral custom, that no one should see the sun, but should go outside the caverns only during the night; and

it is for this reason that the poet speaks of them as follows: 'And never does the shining sun look upon them'; but later on the Cimmerians were destroyed by a certain King, because the response of the oracle did not turn out in his favor; the seat of the oracle, however, still endures, although it has been removed to another place.

This other place seems to have been located. A passage, believed to be the corridor of the Cumaean Sibyl's sanctuary, has

been discovered, cut through solid rock near the top of the bluff above the sea. As, step by carefully placed step, I traversed the long, dark tunnel, dimly lit by apertures in the rock to the west, and approached the cave, green with oxidized copper, at its end, I was in a believing mood.

The number of ancient Sibyls, and their origins, is disputed—Varro names ten; in the Sistine Chapel, Michelangelo depicts six. His Cumaean Sibyl is an old woman, powerfully framed; her portrayal accords with the legend of the seeress Herophile, born in Asia Minor, who wandered over most of Greece, prophesying at Samos, Colophon, Delos and Delphi before she came to Cumae. Servius tells that Apollo promised her as many years of life as she could hold grains of sand in her hand if she never looked on the soil of her Erythraean home-land again, and that she died when she received a letter closed with a clay seal. Others say that she withered away, having forgotten to ask Apollo for the gift of youth as well as life.

The Romans rated her prophecies so highly that in the time of the Tarquin kings the books in which they were inscribed were moved to Rome and kept for consultation in the Temple of Jupiter.

During Cumae's centuries of independence, her soldiers and sailors gave good accounts of themselves. Cumaean forces checked a major attempted Etruscan expansion in 524 B.C. at Aricia near Rome; as allies, they joined Syracuse in another decisive action, at sea off Cumae in 474. The British Museum displays an Etruscan helmet dedicated to Zeus at Olympia by the Syracusan leader; it is inscribed: "Hiero, son of Deinomenes, and the Syracusans, to Zeus, from the Etruscans at Cumae." In his First Pythian ode, Pindar exalts the encounter.

Some fifty years thereafter, Cumae fell to the local tribe of

Samnites; in 334, when it became a Roman city, it was granted special privileges because of the veneration Romans felt for the Cumaean Sibyl.

In Sicily, Naxos too maintained a long primacy, chiefly ceremonial in nature, due to its Temple of Apollo Archegetes (the leader). Through the years, all important missions arriving at or leaving the island came to sacrifice there before proceeding further.

Naxos itself, narrowly confined between Aetna and the sea, did not become a focus of power, but Catana and Leontini, its two foundations further south in the great plain of the Simeto River, did. Excavations at Naxos show a sturdy wall and a pottery kiln that verifies local production supplementing the supply of vases imported from Greece. Hoards of coins have also been found: the fifth-century Naxian tetradrachma with a crouching Silenus is among the most beautiful in all the wealth of Sicily.

In the patchwork of western Greek settlements, Euboeian colonists thus appear in many places. Along with the Athenians, the inhabitants of the Cyclades, and the cities of the northern Asia Minor coast, they belonged to the Ionian strain of Greeks; this racial tie accounted alike for some of their future alliances and

for some of their lasting antipathies to adjacent colonies founded by the Dorian strain.

Other early colonizers came from eastern shores of the Mediterranean. In the eighth century, the island of Rhodes dispatched settlements to Spain and Gaul. After the conquests of the Lydian King Croesus in Asia Minor, citizens of Colophon who wanted to live under their own institutions established Siris in the instep of the Italian boot, a colony that shortly succumbed to attack by later comers.

Phocaea, a city north of Smyrna, founded some half dozen centers in the extreme western Mediterranean, among them Massalia (Marseilles). This outpost at the mouth of the Rhône became the port through which the tribes of Gaul experienced the Hellenizing influence of Greek trade—the great bronze crater of Vix, now at Châtillon-sur-Seine, was treasured in a sixth century grave of a Gallic lady of high degree.

The whole city of Phocaea moved west after the Persian conquest of Asia Minor, first to Alalia on Corsica, and then, when ejected by Punic and Etruscan forces, to the Greek-dominated west coast of Southern Italy at Elea. Later known as Velia, this city developed into a center of philosophic learning; it was the home of the inventor of dialectic, Zeno, and the philosophers Xenophanes and Parmenides. Plato reports a conversation between Socrates, Zeno and Parmenides in his dialogue, *Parmenides.*

Refugees from Greek cities that had been conquered and destroyed by other Greeks likewise became settlers. After a prolonged campaign in the western Peloponnese, the Spartans expelled the Messenians from their capital; in turn, the Messenians took over the Euboeian settlements on either side of the Straits, and renamed Zankle, Messana (Messina).

66   Likewise related to this Spartan conquest is the legend of the

founding of Taras (Tarentum, Taranto) on the inside of the heel of the Italian boot. During the Spartans' absence in the Messenian war, slaves and others fathered on the Spartan women sons who became known as the Partheneioi (offspring of maidens). Rejected at home, they sought their fortunes abroad, with Phalanthus as their leader.

Pausanias says that, on setting out, Phalanthus was told by the Delphic oracle

> that he would gain a country and a city when he should feel rain under a cloudless sky (*aithra*) . . . . . But when, in spite of his victories over the barbarians, he could not take any of their cities . . . . . he remembered the oracle, and thought that the god had predicted what could never come to pass . . . . . In his despondency his wife, who had followed him from home, caressed him: in particular she laid his head on her lap and loused him; and somehow for the love she bore him, she fell a-weeping to see that his fortunes were at a standstill. Now, as she shed tears freely and wetted her husband's head, he perceived the meaning of the oracle, for his wife's name was 'Aethra'; and that very night he took Tarentum, the greatest and wealthiest of all the cities of the barbarians on the sea.

The city's fine harbor was a natural first-and-last port of call for shipping to and from Greece, and its merchants developed as a specialty the famous purple dye originated by the Phoenicians: murex, the crustacean whose shell supplied both the dye and a frequent motif for the decoration of early vases, was plentiful in nearby waters.

West of Taras around the instep of the Italian boot were three colonies founded by Achaeans from the southern coast of the Gulf of Corinth: Metapontum, Sybaris, Croton. Their most con-   *67* spicuous remaining ruin is Metapontum's sixth century temple of Hera: of the forty-eight columns of its colonnade, fifteen stand. Because of its fine harbor, Croton has been heavily overlaid by later cities; there, only a single column on a nearby promontory remains in erect evidence of one of Hera's most frequented sanctuaries in Greek Italy, a temple decorated, in its heyday, with paintings by Zeuxis.

Sybaritic luxury became a byword—the name survived to enter the English language as an adjective without a capital. Yet until the present decade, the very site of Sybaris was a matter for archaeological probing: at the end of the sixth century the Crotonians not only reduced it to complete ruin but diverted the river Krathis to obliterate the last trace. Excavations are now in process near Rosano di Calabria. In view of the completeness of its disappearance, it is ironic that the best preserved of Italy's Greek cities is that founded by the Sybarites to give them direct overland access to the west coast, the city then called Poseidonia but renamed Paestum by the Romans and so known today.

The remnants of the Sybarite population fled inland: some sixty years later their descendants joined with other Greeks in the Panhellenic foundation on their former territory sponsored by Pericles and named Thurii. This town was laid out by the town planner Hippodamus of Miletus. Herodotus wrote much of his *History* and died there.

Croton had many fames. In the sixth century Pythagoras came from his native Samos to make it a renowned center of learning. He established the discipline of geometry, demonstrated the mathematical nature of the musical scale, invented the term "philosopher," and developed a system of thought which Timaeus and Aristoxenes wrote down two hundred years later and Plato drew

68 on in his *Timaeus, Republic* and *Laws*. His philosophy became

the basis of a cult with a corporate brotherhood; Croton was governed by its intellectuals in a manner comparable to the government of the Calvinists at Geneva.

As a producer of great athletes, the city was likewise renowned throughout the Mediterranean world: the Crotonian wrestler Milon was said to have amassed no less than thirty-one crowns at the four Great Games of Greece, Olympia, Delphi, the Isthmus and Nemea. Describing the monuments to winners at Olympia, Pausanias reports:

> The statue of Milo, son of Diotimus, is by Dameas, also a native of Crotona . . . . . It is said that Milo carried his own statue into the Altis. His feats with the pomegranate and the quoit are also narrated. He would hold a pomegranate so fast that no one could wrest it from his hand, yet so daintily that he did not crush it; again he used to stand on a greased quoit, and jeer at those who charged at him and tried to push him off it. Other exhibitions of his were these. He would tie a cord round his brow like a fillet or crown; then, holding in his breath and filling the veins in his head with blood, he would, by the strength of his veins, burst the cord in two. It is said, too, that he would let down at his side his upper right arm from the shoulder to the elbow, and stretch out straight the lower arm from the elbow, so that the thumb was uppermost and the other fingers in a row; in this position then the little finger was lowest, and no one could stir it by any exertion of strength.

Croton's third fame came from its great physicians, one of whom, according to Herodotus, caused the Persian King Darius to accelerate his effort to conquer Greece. This Demokedes left home because of a harsh father; he practiced his art, at rising fees, first at Aegina, then at Athens, then at Samos, where Polykrates ruled.

Rush of Arrival

In an attempt to capture the riches of Samos, the Persian king's viceroy at Sardis murdered Polykrates and enslaved Demokedes. But shortly thereafter, he himself fell out of royal favor and was put to death. His slaves were brought to Susa, the Great King's capital. Herodotus continues:

> Not long after this, it happened that Darius, while hunting, twisted his foot in dismounting from his horse, so violently that the ball of the ankle joint was dislocated from its socket. Darius called in the first physicians of Egypt, whom he had till now kept near his person; who, by their forcible wrenching of the foot, did but make the hurt worse; and for seven days and nights the king could get no sleep for the pain. On the eighth day he was in very evil case; then someone, who had heard in Sardis of the skill of Democedes of Croton, told the king of him. . . . . . .

Demokedes at first denied he was a physician, but when the king insisted he try his skill:

> Democedes applied Greek remedies and used gentleness instead of the Egyptians' violence; whereby he made the king able to sleep and in a little while recovered him of his hurt, though Darius had had no hope of regaining the use of his foot. After this, Darius rewarded him with a gift of two pairs of golden fetters. "Is it your purpose," Democedes asked, "to double my pains for making you whole?" Darius, pleased by his wit, sent him to the king's wives. The eunuchs brought him to the women, saying, "This is he who saved the king's life"; whereupon each of them took a vessel and, scooping with it from a chest full of gold, so richly rewarded the physician that the servant, whose name was Sciton, collected a very great sum of gold by following and gleaning the staters that fell from the vessels . . . . . .

So now for having healed Darius at Susa Democedes had a very great house and ate at the king's table; all was his except only permission to return to his Greek home.

Then the king's wife Atossa developed a cyst on her breast, and Demokedes saw an opportunity. As a favor for curing it, he urged her to persuade Darius to undertake an expedition.

"Sire, you are a mighty ruler," [she said,] "why sit you idle, winning neither new dominions or new power for your Persians?"

Darius replied:

"What you say I am already minded to do. I am resolved to make a bridge from this to the other continent and so lead an army against the Scythians . . . ."

Atossa countered:

"Forbear for the nonce to attack the Scythians; you will find them whenever you so desire; nay, rather, I pray you, march against Hellas. I have heard of Laconian and Argive and Attic and Corinthian women, and would fain have them for handmaidens. There is a man by you who is fitter than any other to instruct and guide you in all matters concerning Hellas; I mean the physician who healed your foot."

On two triremes, followed by a cargo ship laden with gifts for Demokedes' relatives, Darius dispatched his physician and fifteen Persian nobles to coast along the shores of Hellas, making careful surveys. When they reached Taras, Demokedes persuaded the king to arrest the Persians as spies and take the steering gear off their ships, while he left for home.

The Persians appeared at Croton after regaining their freedom, but the Crotonians refused to give up their townsman. Knowing the Persians' awe of the might of Milon, Demokedes had pru- 71 dently affianced himself to Milon's daughter, "seeking this match," says Herodotus, "and paying a great sum for it." So Demokedes remained in his native city, while, after further adventures and vicissitudes, the Persian nobles returned to Susa and presented Darius with their inventory of the coasts of Greece. In 490, the great king built his "bridge from this to the other continent", and advanced to Marathon.

Midway down the Italian toe was another Achaean colony, Caulonia, of which little remains; west of it is the namesake settlement placed by Lokrians from middle mainland Greece.

Lokri's recovered ruins are in several locations. Near the sea, a large area of streets, temples and houses includes one of the two wholly Ionic sanctuaries in Magna Graecia—the other was at Hipponion, a Lokrian colony on the west Italian coast. Twin statues, perhaps akroteria, from this temple, portraying Castor and Pollux with mounts supported by sea-monsters, are in the museum at Naples.

Further inland at Casa Marfioli a Doric temple was topped by the large akroterion now in the museum at Reggio di Calabria.

I stopped at Reggio especially to see this horseman, whose mount is supported by a sphinx. As I approached the museum, workmen with wheelbarrows gave clear warning that a reconstruction was in progress; nevertheless, I presented myself to the guard at opening time.

The sound of our protracted conversation apparently penetrated the interior; a large, authoritative gentleman emerged and inspected me. "Tourist?" he inquired, dubiously.

Negation and indignation merged in my answer: "Certainly not! Journalist!"

He let me in. Forms were filled out for photographic authorization. Produced for identification, the glorious technicolor of my

72

White House press pass went from hand to hand. Over planks and past wet cement patches I was led to the akroterion. Three men turned its considerable bulk so that it would stand in the best light.

Along with heartfelt thanks, I expressed a determination to come back when all was finished and see the entire collection, especially the terra cotta reliefs of Hades and Persephone, Aphrodite and Hermes, Demeter and Dionysos, and the pomegranate pickers. Meanwhile I would visit Lokri.

At the station, I found a man with a car. We began with the settlement near the shore. Then we started across country to Lokri's theater. First we followed a track through an ancient olive grove. Then we negotiated our way in low gear between village walls along a street whose width was approximately that 73 of the vehicle. Grazing plaster, we made a right turn. Beyond the village, another track traced its way between more olive trees. It ended, and there was the theater of Epizephyrian Lokri, far from everywhere, dreaming in the afternoon sun. The scene was a bucolic idyll, such as Theocritus longed for and praised:

Grant that towns which the hands of foes have wasted utterly be peopled again by their ancient masters. May these till fertile fields, while sheep in countless thousands grow fat upon the pastures and bleat over the plain, and cattle gathering in their herds to the homestead speed the twilight traveller on his way. May the fallows be worked for seed-time while the cicada overhead, watching the shepherds in the sun, makes music in the foliage of trees. May spiders spin their delicate webs over armour, and the cry of onset be no more even named.

But the Greek colonies in the west that became the makers of history were those founded on the southern part of the east coast and the eastern part of the south coast of Sicily, chiefly by Dorian Greeks.

In the eighth century, arriving Megarans from north of the Isthmus of Corinth made favorable terms with the nearby Sikels and set themselves up at Megara Hyblaea below Leontini. A hundred years later, in 628, their descendants, with reinforcements from home, established Selinus (Selinunte) on the south coast, the westernmost of Greek Sicilian colonies.

About 689, Rhodians and Cretans founded Gela on the south coast; a hundred years later, the Geloans planted Akragas on the next major city-site to the west.

The greatest of the cities was a colony of Corinth. In 734, a year after the establishment of Naxos, Corinthian settlers drove out and replaced the Sikels on the island of Ortygia and established Syracuse, which in turn colonized Acrae (Piazza Acreidae), Casmenae and Camarina to dominate the entire southeast corner of Sicily.

On Ortygia and the adjacent mainland shore, around the bays of a natural double harbor, the settlers placed what became the ranking Greek city of the west, the city that at the height of the classical period was second in the Greek world only to Athens itself. Syracuse was the pivot of Greek history: the decisive battle in the Ionian-Dorian conflict that long engaged Ionian Athens and Dorian Corinth and Sparta took place around and in its harbor.

Earlier, the Corinthians had planted a colony on Korkyra (Corfu), between the west coast of Greece and the Italian heel. From this large and fruitful island, outbound or return journeys of all shipping to or from the west could be effectively monitored. Greek sailors preferred to travel by day and beach their ships at   75 night: cargoes for Magna Graecia therefore coasted along the shores of Epirus, thence via Korkyra across the Adriatic to the eastern tip of Italy and so forward to their destinations. Whoever rivalled Corinth had to reckon also with the power of this strategic outpost.

But in the mid-fifth century, Corinth and her colony fell out. Athens promptly offered the colony a new alliance. Its consummation greatly expedited the coming of the Peloponnesian War.

CHAPTER V

Hera's Italian Votive

In the entire Greek world, only the Hephaesteion in Athens and the 'Concordia' at Agrigento in Sicily stand more intact than the group of three great sanctuaries at Paestum, sixty miles south of Naples. Nowhere else is there so complete a row of comparable buildings.

The two most impressive of these shrines, and a third at Paestum's adjacent seaport at the mouth of the River Sele, were all dedicated to Hera.

For once, Zeus (Jupiter) seems to have kept a promise to his spouse. In the closing pages of the *Aeneid,* in exasperation, the

Hera's Italian Votive

Olympian thunderer informs his irritating consort that he has had enough.

> *No more of the hidden rancour that so consumes you, the sullen*
> *Recriminations your sweet lips have troubled me with so often!*
> *This is the end, I say. You had power to harry the Trojans*
> *All over lands and seas, to kindle accursed war,*
> *Bring tragic disgrace on a king's home and drape a betrothal in*
> *   mourning.*
> *I forbid you to carry the feud any further . . . .*

Determined to bargain even in defeat, Hera (Juno) makes it a condition of her obedience that the Trojans shall not be allowed to absorb the Latins; rather, they shall assume the Latins' name:

> *Let it be Latium forever, and the kings be Alban kings;*
> *Let the line be Roman, the qualities making it great be Italian.*

Zeus, yielding a minor point to gain a major purpose, accedes, and adds the promise that in the Italian land she shall have special honor:

> *. . . . . All will be Latins, speaking*
> *One tongue. From this blend of Italian and Trojan blood shall arise*
> *A people surpassing all men, nay even the gods, in godliness.*
> *No other nation on earth will pay such reverence to Juno.*

In Paestum, from tremendous edifice in stone to tiny figurine in terra cotta, Hera is venerated; Strabo says that her temple at the city's port was founded by Jason and the Argonauts.

As yet, only a fraction of the ancient city is uncovered. The center, with its sacred way, sanctuaries and altars, Roman amphitheater, market areas, has been excavated, and the new Museum exhibits a wealth of finds. But the residential sections lie under green fields.

It is easy to visualize the extent of the classical settlement because the city walls are still there. Forming a rough rectangle, entered by four gates, they are some three miles in circumference, fifteen to twenty-one feet thick and in places as much as forty-five feet high. Their firmly fitted blocks are surmounted by towers, some round, some square, like those on the walls built by Epaminondas at Messene in the Peloponnese. The stonework compares with that of Timoleon's slightly later fortifications at Gela in Sicily.

Entering through the east gate, arched over by the Romans, I walked alongside spring fields lush with the intense green of winter wheat and bordered by Campanian umbrella pines. To my left was an ancient estate, its tan-plastered, red-tiled house surrounded by fruited orange and lemon trees behind a high wall. I observed that centuries ago a cultivator had heightened a Greek watch tower with the perforated stone-work of a columbarium.

All of this farm was once Paestum; to the west, beyond the shining stones of the city's sacred way, is a comparable unexplored area.

The earliest temple in the sacred precinct at the southern end of the excavations dates from the middle of the sixth century B.C. Its architecture is archaic Doric, with pillars set directly on the stylobate—since Doric columns developed from earlier wooden ones, they never had bases. The avoidance of rectilinear rigidity that gives classical Greek temples their lightness and grace is already evident, if still a little awkward: the columns swell and then taper markedly toward the top, where a very flat echinus underlies a narrow abacus, looking rather like a ball of dough with a heavy weight on it.

Three of the columns of the west end of this temple are exceptional in that the echinus is decorated. The designs are of leaves; leaves and palmettos; alternating lotus and roses. (The twice-blooming roses of Paestum were celebrated.)

More unusual still is the arrangement of the interior of this sanctuary. The classic plan for a large temple provides three to five steps from the ground to the stylobate, where a columned, covered walkway, the peristyle, permitted worshippers from the public at large to stroll around the exterior walls. Within these walls was the inner sanctum, where the god enjoyed his privacy except for the ministering priest. On the north and south sides of the peristyle, the walls were solid. To the east was a columned

opening, the pronaos, a vestibule through which one looked into the naos or cella, the room containing the statue of the god. At the west end, a similar columned entrance led into the opistho-domos or thesauros, the treasury in which were kept the votives offered by worshippers. Practically without exception—Bassae in the Peloponnese is an exception—temples were oriented along an east-west axis. The animal sacrifices were performed at low altars located in front of the temple at the east end.

The unusual feature of Paestum's oldest temple is the division of its central area by a row of columns running east and west down the middle. Temples were usually dedicated to a single god, though Demeter and Persephone, and Ares and Aphrodite were not infrequent combinations, and the Erechtheion at Athens honored both Poseidon and Athena. In this case separate sanc-tuaries were included in the same building. But present research indicates that the dedication of Paestum's oldest temple was ex-clusively to Hera.

The most complete of the temples stands just north of the ear-liest; by looking toward the former through the columns of the latter one can see the changes that occurred in the transition from the archaic to the classic Doric style. The newer columns have much less swelling, the echinus is much less flat.

Dating from about 450 B.C., this middle temple, earlier thought to be Poseidon's, just precedes the Parthenon, on which work was begun in 447; it is almost exactly contemporary with the He-phaesteion. The modifications of straight lines have become much more subtle: the stylobate is slightly curved, the columns are in-clined inward. The middle columns are round and slightly larger than the others; the corner ones are elliptical.

According to classical rule, the number of columns on the sides of a temple should be twice the number of those on the ends,

plus one—the Parthenon has eight and seventeen, the Hephaesteion six and thirteen. Two of the Paestum temples, however, have even numbers of columns on their sides. The temple of 450 B.C. has fourteen, with six on the ends; that with the inner division has eighteen on the sides and nine on the ends—its entrance therefore could not have been centered.

The temple of 450 B.C. is exceptional in Italy in having two-storeyed rows of inner columns; the arrangement is similar to the temple of Aphaia at Aegina in Greece, and Hera at Agrigento in Sicily. To the right of the naos are three steps of a flight that led up to the room above the cella; to the left, a small room that may have been for the priest in Roman times, comparable to similar rooms in Egypt. The flat roof over the cella formed a floor for the hall or adyton above it; the flat ceiling supported by the two-storey columns was in turn topped by a pitched roof of huge clay

tiles laid on beams and covering the entire building; a number of tiles lie on the ground intact.

The third temple is in another sacred precinct at the north end of the excavated area, beyond the Roman forum and amphitheater. It is a complex structure dating from about 510 B.C. and now thought to have been dedicated to Athena. The columns of its peristyle, six in front, thirteen on the sides, are archaic Doric, but their necks are decorated with mouldings which form a graceful transition to an echinus whose shape is much closer to the classic than to the archaic form. The eight columns of the pronaos are in the Ionic style.

The entablature of this temple has been subjected to Roman reconstruction: courses of narrow red brick distort its proportions.

The marked differences in the color of the three temples—the northern one is much the lightest, the middle one a deep honey-color—might encourage an assumption that the limestone of which they are constructed came from different quarries. This is not the case; the variation is a variation in the quantity of iron particles in the stone—the honey color is the result of oxidization. Since temples built of limestone were covered with white plaster to make them look like marble, their builders found such differences immaterial.

Paestum was preserved by a massive geologic subsidence followed by flooding in the latter part of the first millenium A.D. From the beginning, the site had had water on three sides: with mountains at its back it lies on a flat coastal plain between two east-to-west flowing rivers, the Sele to the north, the Salso to the south.

As the land sank, brackish water accumulated, creeping up temple walls, rising over sacrificial altars, flooding the Roman amphitheater, until the city was submerged to a depth of some fifteen feet. (The subsidence of historic times was not the first; marine deposits of the geologic past layer the limestone from which the temples are built.) Malaria came in, people moved out. Rank swamp-vegetation sprouted unchecked, obscuring the unsubmerged superstructures.

For centuries, sluggish waters etched their levels on upright surfaces. Tiny crustaceans imbedded themselves in pock-marks and crannies in the submerged stone. In the Roman area of the city, a metope of a second-century B.C. temple shows a warrior with upraised shield. Stuck in the angle between the reverse side of the shield and the stone background is an ancient snail shell.

The city was lost to sight until 1752, when from his capital at Naples Charles III, Bourbon King of the Two Sicilies, ordered construction of a north-south coastal coach road along the peninsula. The infested swamp lay in its path. As the engineers pushed in, Paestum reappeared.

Since then, drainage throughout the region has restored the land to agriculture. After World War II an intensive campaign eliminated malaria.

In addition to its group of temples, Paestum has in its Museum metopes that are unique in Italy. Metopes are the carved blocks set between the triglyphs of a temple's entablature to provide exterior decoration. They parallel the frieze around the inside wall of the peristyle. In the surviving architecture of Greece proper, they occur frequently, but not in the architecture of Magna Graecia. Only at Selinunte in Sicily and Paestum in Italy have any been discovered.

None were found on Paestum's three great temples, but a treasure trove of fifty-seven was uncovered at the city's port at the mouth of the Sele River.

One series of twelve adorned the Heraeion built at the end of the sixth century; a chorus leader directs pairs of girls in a sacred dance. The difference between the treatment of these dancers' faces and their dress contributes to speculation about the origins of Greek sculpture. The technique of carving statues was presumably transplanted from Egypt—with one exception. On Egyptian statues the draperies of women as well as men permissably left much of the body exposed. Greek sculptors of youths discarded the loin-cloths usual among Egyptians; from the first, kouroi were presented entirely nude. But Greek social mores long required statues of women to be fully covered, with only feet, arms and face exposed. (An Athenian legend recounts how Praxiteles, in the

88

mid-fourth century, was brought before the Areopagus morals court for carving a woman's figure in the nude. His model had been Phryne, his mistress. In his defense, her beauty was unveiled before the judges. They concluded that no offence had occurred.)

Greek sculptors of the early centuries therefore had to carve peplum and chiton and himation without conventional models, looking directly at what they saw. Whoever carved the Paestum reliefs of dancers captured the flow of line in their draperies even as the sculptors who carved the three-dimensional korae of the Acropolis Museum; the sweep of the dancing maidens' garments contrasts with their traditional archaic profiles.

The other series of Sele metopes, thirty-five of them, came from a treasury. They are now mounted where they can be studied at suitable height. Their quality varies: the work of different artists, the designs on eleven of them are only sketched, with the carving left incomplete. Their subjects range widely over mythology, including an engaging centaur and a Herakles with two trussed Cyclops hanging head down from a pole across his shoulders. Most arresting is the flight of two forceful maidens, rigidly in step.

Elsewhere in the Museum, the remarkably complete statue of a seated god, perhaps Zeus, still retains much of its original color on face and beard, yellow chiton and red himation; it invites comparison with the statues from the archaic temple of Athena Polias in the Acropolis Museum. The many terra cotta figurines at Paestum—and more from these same excavations are exhibited at Naples—complement the great temples by witnessing the small human piety of individual worshippers.

Paestum enjoyed two periods of prominence. It maintained its independence as Greek for three hundred years from its foundation in the seventh century, then fell to the neighboring Lucan- 89 ians. When they, in turn, were conquered by Rome, the city flourished anew as part of the imperium; during the opening years of the empire it was an ornament of the Augustan Age. In his *Georgics*, Vergil writes with nostalgia:

> *Indeed, were it not that already my work has made its landfall*
> *And I shorten sail and eagerly steer for the harbour mouth,*
> *I'd sing perhaps of rich gardens, their planning and cultivation,*
> *The rose beds of Paestum that bloom twice in a year,*
> *The way endive rejoices to drink from a rivulet,*
> *The bank all green with celery, the cucumber snaking*
> *Amid the grass and swelling to greatness; I'd not forget*
> *Late flowering narcissus or gum-arabic's ringlet shoots,*
> *Pale ivy, shore loving myrtle.*

CHAPTER VI

Two Vigilant Enemies

Segesta, city of the Elymian aborigines, lies near the western end of the north Sicilian coast. Directly below it on the south coast lies Selinunte, the city that was the westernmost out-post of Greek colonization. In the history of Greek Sicily,—and indeed of all Greece,—the unceasing enmity between these two took on proportions far greater than those of a local rivalry.

I went first to Segesta. The train from Palermo paused to let me off, then hurried west to Trapani. Only a few steps from the station, I was walking between fields. The uphill road led over a bridge where a river hurried seaward, past a spring channeled into a trough where a countryman was watering his donkey, around the shoulder of the long hill that had cut off my distant glimpse. Mine was the millenial pace by which travellers would have come when Segesta—Egesta, they called it then,—was one of the major centers of power in non-Greek Sicily.

Long before Alexander the Great brought culture at the sword-point to the empires of Asia Minor, the Hellenization of non-Greeks was an accomplished fact in Sicily. In the western as in the eastern Mediterranean the local peoples adopted Greek customs, imitated Greek architecture. Segesta, though often a Greek ally, was never a Greek possession. Yet among examples of classical architecture in Sicily, Segesta's temple yields in beauty to none whose provenance is more authentically Greek.

It stands alone. On its own hill, on the hills on either side, on the mountain across the gorge to the west, the land is wild pasture. Sparse green, scattered with stone, and sheer grey rock are the background colors, contrasting with the tawny edifice.

In incompleteness, the temple is complete. What is seen now is very probably all that was ever there—a Doric peristyle, entire even to its pediments, but with no cella, columns, or indeed stylobate within. It is as though a major sanctuary had been begun, and the great drums of the outer columns set in place, but further work, even the fluting of the columns, deferred to total abandonment.

Hence the colonnade's purity of line is obscured by no inner clutter of partly fallen walls; in the spring, the floor is paved with a natural stylobate of dwarf white daisy-flowers.

The columns, set on square bases in a departure from Doric style, taper as they rise; at their necks, four incised lines decorate the transition to an upcurving echinus; on the abacus, small squares of stone project at the four corners. Finished triglyphs enhance the entablature.

Openings have been left in the stylobate on both sides of the southwest corner column, and between the fourth and fifth and the ninth and tenth columns on the south side. Were these to bring in material for the interior? Why should completion of the stylobate and erection of the inner walls and columns not have been accomplished first, before enclosing the space with the peristyle? The empty temple is full of unanswered questions.

Where, too, were Segesta's other sanctuaries? The loneliness of this one, its pervading presence alike when seen from a distance in the empty landscape and when the wild surrounding country is viewed through its colonnades, give it a quality close to unique —Apollo's temple at Bassae is the other sanctuary of the Greek world that evokes a comparable experience.

93

For hours I stayed in the temple, watching the early light quicken the honey-colored stone of the eastern exposure. As the sun swung southward, it laid a flat peristyle of sharp-cut shadow on the white daisy stylobate.

Perhaps Segesta had more than one sacred precinct; on the opposite hill from the peristyle, the Elymians had an acropolis above their theater. The latter is well-preserved, the former, identifiable. A deep valley and about a mile of road separate them from the existing temple—the Segestaeans shared the Greek's delight in looking at one beautiful building from another some distance away.

Among Segesta's statues was a famous image of Artemis. In the late classical period, the Carthaginians who overwhelmed the city removed it along with other spoils. At the end of the Third Punic War, the Roman general Scipio Africanus destroyed Carthage and restored the statue to Segesta—the city was by that time allied to Rome. But in the first century B.C. a corrupt Roman governor of Sicily, Gaius Verres, who systematically ravaged the entire island, stole it away again.

Cicero, who himself had been a civil servant in the island, came to Enna (a tablet marks his house-site) and prepared on behalf of the Sicilian people a documented charge against this man. At the start of Book IV of his Second Verrine Oration, he describes what happened here:

> There is, gentlemen, a very ancient town in Sicily named Segesta; it is alleged to have been founded by Aeneas, when he had fled from Troy and arrived in our part of the world; and the Segestans in consequence regard themselves as bound to Rome not only by permanent alliance and friendship but also by ties of blood. Long ago, when Segesta was independently at war with Carthage

on its own account, the town was assaulted, captured and destroyed
by the Carthaginians, and everything in it that might add to the
beauty of the city of Carthage was carried away thither. There was
in the town a bronze image of Diana, regarded from very ancient
times as highly sacred, and moreover, a work of art of extremely
fine workmanship. Its removal to Carthage was no more than a
change of home and worshippers; the reverence formerly felt for it
remained, for its exceptional beauty made even an enemy people
feel it worthy of the most devout adoration. In the third Punic War,
some centuries later, Publius Scipio captured Carthage. In the hour
of victory . . . . knowing that Sicily had repeatedly . . . . been
ravaged by the Carthaginians, he called all the Sicilians together,
and ordered a general search to be made, promising to do his utmost for the restoration to the several communities of all that was
once theirs . . . . It was at this time that the utmost care was taken
to return to the Segestans the very statue of Diana that I speak of;
it was brought back to their town, and set up once more in its
ancient home, amid the loud rejoicings of grateful citizens . . . .
The figure, draped in a long robe, was of great size and height; but
in spite of its dimensions, it well suggested the youthful grace of a
maiden, with quiver hung from one shoulder, bow in the left hand,
and the right hand holding forth a blazing torch. No sooner had
yonder enemy of all religion and plunderer of all sacred things
beheld it than his heart was kindled with the flames of insane desire, as though that torch had actually smitten him; he ordered the
magistrates to take it down and give it to him, as the greatest favour
they could confer on him. They replied that this would be a wicked
thing for them to do, and that extreme fear of legal punishment, as
well as the strongest of religious motives, forbade them to do it.
Verres besought and threatened them by turns, seeking now to
encourage and now to frighten them . . . . . Verres then proceeded
to impose on Segesta greater burdens than on any other place in
Sicily in the way of requisitioning sailors and rowers, or supplies of

95

corn—considerably more than they were capable of bearing. In addition, he would summon their magistrates to his presence, sending for their best and most distinguished men, and dragging them round all the assize-towns of the province; he would tell each man severally that he would ruin him, and all of them together that he meant to smash their community to pieces. And thus, in the end, crushed by their many sufferings and fears, the Segestans agreed that the governor's command should be obeyed. Amid the grief and lamentation of the whole community, with tears and cries of grief from every man and every woman in it, a contract was authorized for the removal of the image of Diana. Mark now the strength of religious feeling this evoked at Segesta. Gentlemen, let me assure you that not one person could be found, neither free man nor slave, neither citizen nor immigrant, who would venture to lay hands upon that statue; some foreign labourers were got in from Lilybaeum, who, knowing nothing of the affair or its religious bearings, for a certain sum of money ultimately removed it. As it was being carried out of the town, you can imagine the crowd of women that gathered, and the tears of the older people, some of whom could still remember the day when this same Diana had been brought back from Carthage to Segesta, carrying with it the news of the Roman victory. What a difference they would feel between now and then! Then, the illustrious commander of the Roman armies was bringing the god of Segesta, recovered from an enemy city, back to its own home: now, an evil and filthy Roman governor was committing the awful sin of carrying off that same god from an allied and friendly city. No story is better known throughout Sicily than that of how, when Diana was being borne out of the town, all the matrons and maidens of Segesta flocked to the spot, anointed her with perfumes, covered her with garlands and flowers, and burning incense and spices escorted her to the frontier of their land.

Did the statue stand on the high point of the city, a signal to travellers like that of Athena Polias at Athens or Hera at Syracuse? About midday I started toward the acropolis, intending to munch my bread and cheese looking across to the templed hill.

The acropolis is considerably higher than the temple; after I left the road, the ground was strewn with shards—sections of columns, a hollow trough, large stones that might have been pieces of a cornice, innumerable fragments of pottery, bits of Roman brick.

At the top was a formidable citadel; trenches prepared for last-ditch battle can still be traced around the summit. To the east, the gorge of the Crimisos river parallels that of the stream to the west of the temple; in all directions, the land falls off in great sweeping views of plain and hill. At my level, a hawk glided with set wings; it was doubled, far below, by a wide-arcing shadow on the land.

Two Vigilant Enemies

Wheat fields and sprouting vineyards striped the rolling plains with dark and pale green rectangles. Here and there, made tiny by distance, flocks of sheep moved as dots upon the hills.

The wind was strong from the west—no windbreak intervenes between Segesta and Mount Eryx. Hazy-edged sea-mist, compressed into cloud, began to flow by, spreading gray over the green landscape.

As the mist turned to rain, I hurried downhill to take shelter in the theater.

Viewed from the inside, the theater is thoroughly Greek, with no more modification than usually took place in such theaters in Roman times: on the stage side, the circle of the orchestra is cut by a stone skene and other buildings; a channel behind the skene runs under the theater floor. Twenty courses of seats, with access to them by the steps of three tilted corridors, rise to a broad ambulatory aisle, above which the stones of further seats lie in disarray. The vertical risers from seat to seat have curved profiles.

The stone has much pink in it, enhanced by contrast with yellow and black lichens. The rain brightened all colors.

Arched entrances at the butt ends of the stands frame now-clogged corridors that run down under the seats; in one of these, I waited out the shower.

Emerging into restored sunlight, I circled the outside of the theater and observed a difference from Greek models illustrative of what occurs when one people adopts the way of life of another, external to their own experience. From the outside, the Segesta theater looks less like a Greek theater than like another of its foreign derivatives, the modern stadium.

Greek builders found a natural amphitheater in a hill, then deepened and smoothed it to the extent necessary to make a well-proportioned cavea of adequate size. But if the audience at Se-   99 gesta were to face the great north landscape, with the actors casting their shadows behind them, no natural cavea was at hand.

The Segestaeans did not dig very far back into the hill. Instead, they supported the side sections of the cavea by free-standing high stone walls.

Another instance of the architectural adaptation that goes with architectural adoption appears at Morgantina, the great Sikan center in the north-central part of the island. There, Hellenic influence is on display in all the institutions of a great city—theater, sacred precinct, gymnasium with race track, houses with painted walls and mosaic floors, an imposing agora fill a huge shallow bowl on a high hill. The unusual arrangement here is the monumental three-sided stepped area that rises in a half hexagon from the agora at the city's center; it was probably used for meetings of the assembly.

At Morgantina, my do-it-yourself plumber's eye was also caught by an invention improving the water system. I had admired the conduits at Knossos: to expedite flow, they are tapered at the down-grade end according to a principle rediscovered in our own time. But in each section of the main pipe that brought water to Morgantina from still higher in the hills, on the top surface, is a lozenge-shaped insert. Three indentations in the clay permit easy grasp by thumb and forefingers. When the pipe became clogged, removal of the lozenge made cleaning easy.

By the time the sun had moved to the west I was back at the Segesta temple. Now, the shadow colonnade angled across the stylobate in a new direction.

Through the early afternoon, I had listened to intermittent copper clunking as the neck of a bell-wether somewhere was alternately raised to observe possible danger, lowered to resume nibbling. Above it, like a lark song, lilted the piping of a shepherd boy. Both sounds came closer.

Suddenly, scattered fleeces bounded onto the stylobate, filling the center of the temple. After them strode the shepherd, clucking disapproval.

101

He was about thirteen, stocky and sturdy, black-haired and dark-eyed. The cool wet mountain wind had whipped his cheeks until the blood under the tan coursed bright and warm.

Our talk stumbled like the sound of a sheep-bell, but we managed to understand. I took his picture; when I tried to explain that it would be three months before the prints would reach him, I signalled the passage of the fortunately visible moon, held up three fingers. He nodded happily, and held up four fingers to show he would like to have four prints.

I pulled out my pencil and notebook, held them toward him so he could write his address and his name.

The happiness flowed out of his face. He dropped his eyes: "I don't know how."

Quickly, I covered his incapacity: "Just say it, I'll write."

I asked him to play his flute, and especially to play the phrase with which he quietened his ewes.

In the bag slung over his shoulder, he had three pipes of hollow reed. Each had six round holes for stops; their edges and the bottom of the pipe had been charred. As he played, one finger partly

covered the flute's lower end. The sound was as liquid as the stream in which the reed had grown.

Selinunte, Segesta's opponent on the south coast, like its adjacent river, took its name from the plant that grows in profusion along its banks. Selinon is sometimes translated as wild celery and sometimes as wild parsley; it looks very little like either. Plutarch mentions the golden selinon plant dedicated at Delphi; in stylized form, it appears on the city's coins.

This metropolis, nine miles south of Castelvetrano, lies, like Paestum, in a broad and fertile plain sloping gently to the Mediterranean—the kind of land that was a rarity on the Greek peninsula. Even the settlement itself was widely spread.

The walled acropolis occupies a rise close to the shore between the mouth of the Selinon and that of a marshy stream to the east; both outlets may have been enlarged for harbors. Five major temples—a seventeen column colonnade of one mid-sixth century structure has been partly re-erected—formed an extensive sanctuary. Behind them and to the sides, houses flanked streets laid out in a regular grid, with two main boulevards crossing at right angles. Hippodamus of Miletus has usually been credited with the invention of town planning, but this arrangement predates him by some hundred years.

Further north, up the hill, a Hellenistic residential section lies outside massive fortifications that include a curtain wall with arched entrances.

The site of the Selinuntine agora is not known, but there were   *103*

sanctuaries at two other locations, each some distance away. To the west, across the river, the popularity of the large early sixth century sanctuary of Demeter is evidenced by finds of thousands of terra cotta votive figurines. The city's cemetery was still further west, and closer to the coast; sixth century steles from these graves are in Palermo's National Museum.

More than a quarter of a mile to the east, set back from the sea at the top of a rise that mounts both from the coast and from the ancient eastern harbor of the acropolis, was another sacred precinct with a row of tremendous temples. One of them, a mid-fifth century Doric structure of great beauty, has within the past decade been re-erected in considerable completeness. The stones of the other two lie where they were riotously hurled by an earth-
104 quake of proportions difficult to visualize. Dramatizing the vio-

lence, a single headless column still protrudes vertically through the tumbled pile.

The dimensions of the largest temple are startling—it was 371 feet long and 177 feet wide; its stylobate covered one and three quarters acres. Its columns—eight on the ends and seventeen on the sides, were built of drums weighing about 100 tons; their base diameter was a little over 11 feet. By contrast to the Parthenon columns that rise just over thirty-four feet, these were some fifty-three feet high.

The temple was begun around 520 B.C., but never finished. A few miles west, at Rocce di Cusa, is the quarry from which its stone was taken: column drums and architraves, never moved to the site, still lie there. One huge drum is in a field part way between the two places, abandoned at the time of the city's destruction.

The opulence of Selinuntine architecture was evident abroad as well as at home: one of the Treasuries at Olympia was erected by the Selinuntines; it contained, according to Pausanias, "an image of Dionysus whereof the face, feet and hands are made of ivory."

At Selinunte, metopes, now to be seen in the National Museum at Palermo, decorated several temples of different periods. The oldest is an archaic portrayal of Europa crossing dolphin-decorated waters from Phoenicia to Crete on the back of Zeus in the form of a bull. It is apparently a fragment from an early shrine dismantled to erect a more ambitious successor; it was preserved through use as a building block. Likewise from the sixth century are reliefs of Herakles and a bull, the sphinx Alata, and a Delphic triad.

The temple whose colonnade has been restored was the source of three mid-sixth century metopes; on them, Apollo drives a quadriga; Perseus, with Athena beside him, slices off the Gorgon head of Medusa; and Herakles stands with two Cyclops hanging   *105* head down on either side of his massive shoulders as in the corresponding sculpture at Paestum. An early fifth century relief presents Eos and Kephalos; fragments from the most crumpled temple include a gigantomachy, the head of a dying warrior, a female figure with lovely drapery.

On four mid-fifth century metopes from the re-erected temple, Herakles unhelmets an Amazon and is about to smite her, Zeus sits with Hera beside him in rare accord, Artemis sets her hounds on the hapless Akteion who came upon her bathing unawares, and the warrior goddess Athena bests a giant. In these reliefs, marble inserts differentiate the women's heads, arms and feet from the sandstone used for the rest of the carving.

ARTEMIDE E ATTEONE

Frieze fragments include two Amazonomachies from the second fifth of the fifth century, and a sixth-century dance comparable to that from Paestum's Sele temple.

The Selinunte excavations disclosed not only these sculptures but many examples of the terra cotta work in which Sicily excelled. At Palermo, a special room contains, in scale, a mounting of the painted terra cotta cornices from the pediment of the re-erected colonnade, complete with fearsome Gorgon's head in the center of the tympanum.

The collection includes many smaller terra cotta Gorgon's heads, bulls' heads, and figurines. Archaeologists pay special attention to the geometrically patterned Protocorinthian vases, some of which appear to be of an earlier date than the 628 B.C. given by Thucydides for the foundation of the city. The vase collection is rich in finds from the next period as well, the Orientalized types whose softly colored bands are decorated with sphinx, lions, bulls, deer and flowers.

Flowers in unbelievable profusion slowed my return from the eastern temples along the road that runs south between fields to skirt the shore. Scarlet poppies; blue anemones; large and small yellow daisies; a blue-and-purple flowered weed similar to Creeping Jenny; yucca; yellow asphodel; thistles with white-striped leaves; white ageratum; a circular raspberry-colored flower; the cerise and purple of a plant of the lupin family, repeated in miniature by the cerise and purple of wild sweet pea; blue pimpernel; and selinon—all in less than a single mile.

In walking it, I had additional reasons for taking my time. As I left the eastern temples, a man trundling a bicycle crossed the road and entered a footpath that cut through the fields of an adjacent farm. It was about noon; he looked as though he might be a farm laborer on his way home to lunch.

Two Vigilant Enemies

Some distance down the path, he shouted to me, signalling that this was the shortest way across to the acropolis, and for me to come. I signalled thanks for the information, turned my back and continued my photography. I preferred the public highway. In Greece, Zeus and all his children are the friends of strangers, but I had not found disinterested attention comparably prevalent in Sicily.

After an interval, I started down the road. I was bound for the beach rather than the acropolis, anyway. When I swept the field with a glance to be sure he was not waiting, nothing showed. But a few steps later, a chance alignment between a gap in the hedge beside me and a gap along the path revealed his head. Presuming himself hidden, he was lying on the ground.

As I walked, I recalled a tale I had heard that morning in Castelvetrano. A famous fifth-century bronze kouros found in Selinunte had long been negligently stored in the mayor's office in the town hall, but a few years ago, the Mafia, in a bravura display of contempt for municipal authority and familiarity with the international black market for antiquities, kidnapped the kouros. Tonight, I decided, I'll send a postcard to a friend who is an avid reader of whodunits based on classical geography with a message in innocuous code: "Something happened today that would have interested My Brother Michael."

Actually, all that my would-be companion wanted was to sell me a bogus coin. Riding his bicycle from the other direction, he shortly showed up on the highway. In Selinunte, the production of antiquities is a recognized local industry, carried on with precision. The molds used are impressions taken from high-quality originals. Perhaps a little more attention should be paid to weight, but the metals, sometimes bronze but sometimes a silver alloy, are allowed to oxidize to a green that gives the appearance of

recent exhumation after long burial. As we talked, in an adjacent field the steady stroke of hand-cultivation with heavy flat-bladed Sicilian hoes suggested imminent discovery. Particularly if neither party is innocent, after suitably-prolonged discussion prices are very reasonable, with costume jewelry as the end result.

Down on the sand, I enjoyed a long lunch at a little seaside restaurant whose windows overlooked the water. I was waiting for the cloudless interval that in the Sicilian spring seems to occur frequently in early afternoon. Soon, the honey color of the restored temple was quickened by the emerging sun.

At the end of the day, I stood in the western peristyle of this temple, and waited. Seen through its columns, the acropolis is backgrounded by the sea. As clouds obscured the afternoon clarity, the sea turned a dull gray streaked with silver. The silver set forth the outline of the distant colonnade in silhouette.

CHAPTER VII

The Magnificent Tyrants

Beloved brightness, loveliest of the cities of mortals,
house of Persephone, you who keep by the banks of Akragas
where the sheep wander, the templed hill—I beseech you, lady,
graciously, in the kindness of men and immortals likewise,
accept from Pytho this garland for splendid Midas;
accept him also.

So sings Pindar, honoring the Akragantine winner of the flute contest at Delphi in 486 B.C.

In all Greek Sicily, the society of the south coast city of Akragas (Agrigento) exhibited most effulgently the effect on a people of   *111* sudden possession of resources on a scale they have not known before.

"Nothing in excess," the motto on Apollo's temple at Delphi, expressed the lean discipline of body and mind forced upon the Greeks of Greece by their environment and made by them into a ranking virtue. Even today, the Greek word for poverty is a strong word; a man wrestles with his field, to bend it into yielding him a living.

The lean men who from the eighth to the sixth century B.C. settled the fruitful fields of Southern Italy and Sicily, and the Western Europeans who from the seventeenth to the twentieth century A.D. migrated to the virgin lands of the Americas shared a common experience: the cornucopia of Demeter was emptied at their feet.

The Akragantines possessed broad acres for flocks and wheat and the olives whose oil they sold to Carthage. They enjoyed in abundance the water that in their homelands was often even scarcer than good land. Pindar's first Olympian ode began:

> *Best of all things is water, but gold, like a gleaming fire*
> *by night, outshines all pride of wealth beside.*

Lying between the Hypsas and Akragas rivers, the city boasted an elaborate system of conduits and drains, part of which can still be seen, and, according to Diodorus,

> an artificial pool outside the city, seven stades in circumference and twenty cubits deep; into this they brought water and ingeniously contrived to produce a multitude of fish of every variety for their public feastings, and with the fish swans spent their time and a vast multitude of every other kind of bird, so that the pool was an object of great delight to gaze upon.

In the midst of this abundance, the Akragantines easily equated the good and the big, the better and the bigger—did they not live in Magna Graecia?

Fronting the southern exposure of the city, which lies at a little distance inland from the sea, the ridge reserved for the main sacred precinct was a mile long. Residential sections wholly covered the spacious hill where Agrigento stands today; above and behind it, the rock called Rupe Atenea lifted temples to Athena and Zeus.

This entire complex was—and in large part is today—surrounded by miles of formidable city walls; eight gates can be identified now. Along streets which like those of Selinunte seem to have been laid out in a regular grid, lived a population that at the time of greatest prosperity numbered some quarter of a million; a large Roman residential area is under excavation now.

That the soft life was available at many social levels may be inferred from a military order issued in the interest of austerity at a time when the city was under siege: it stipulated that soldiers spending the night on guard duty should not have at their posts "more than one mattress, one cover, one sheepskin and two pillows."

Beyond the day-to-day economics of their agricultural products, Akragantines made a specialty of breeding fine horses. Their entries are repeatedly conspicuous in the victors' rosters of the great Greek Games though their athletes won other events as well. In two successive Olympiads, 416 and 412, B.C., Exainetos of Akragas won the foot race in which primacy brought greatest honor. On his return from his second victory, Diodorus declares: "he was conducted into the city in a chariot and in the procession there were, not to speak of other things, three hundred chariots each drawn by two white horses, all the chariots belonging to citi-

113

zens of Akragas." A magnificent coin was forthwith struck in his honor.

Akragas had been founded from Gela and Rhodes; early in the fifth century an alliance, confirmed by marriages, combined the Emmenid family of Akragantine rulers with the Deinomenids of Gela. Gelon and Polyzalus, the eldest and the youngest of the four Deinomenid brothers, married two daughters of Theron of Akragas; Theron married Gelon's niece.

All were horse-fanciers. Their victories were celebrated in marble, bronze and song.

At Olympia, the Geloan Treasury, oldest of such buildings, was newly embellished. Both Gelon and his brother Hieron dedicated memorials to their racing successes, adorned with chariots, in front of the Temple of Zeus.

At Delphi, the monument that Gelon ordered to celebrate a racing victory appears to have been completed after his death by Polyzalus, who altered the inscription on the base to insert his own name. The Charioteer of Delphi was one of its figures.

At Akragas, sculptures of favorite race-horses were numerous; some statues even honored pet birds.

Theron's brother Xenocrates and his son Thrasyboulos won at Delphi in 490, with Thrasyboulos driving; the son won again at the Isthmus some twenty years later. His close friend Pindar celebrated both victories, and sang of the first:

> *Of men living now, Thrasyboulos*
> *comes beyond others to the mark in his father's eyes,*
>
> *and visits his father's brother with fame complete.*
> *He carries wealth with discretion.*
> *The blossom of youth he gathers is nothing violent,*
> *but wise in the devious ways of the Muses.*

To you, Poseidon, shaker of the earth, lord
of the mastering of horses, he comes, with
   mind to please you.
Also his heart, that is gentle
in the mixing of friends,
passes for sweetness the riddled work of
   the bees.

The Magnificent Tyrants

In the 476 Olympiad, the family took double honors; Pindar probably made a voyage to Sicily especially to take part in these celebrations.

Honoring Theron's triumph in the four-horse chariot race, his Second Olympian ode begins:

> My songs, lords of the lyre,
> which of the gods, what hero, what mortal shall we celebrate?
> Zeus has Pisa; but Herakles founded the Olympiad
> out of the spoils of his warfare;
> but Theron, for his victory with chariot-four, is the man
> we must sing now, him of the kind regard to strangers,
> the towering Akragantine,
> choice bud of a high line guarding the city.

Commemorating Hieron's victory in the bareback race for horse and rider, Pindar names the great stallion, Pherenikos:

> . . . . . . They come their ways
> to the magnificent board of Hieron,
>
> who handles the scepter of dooms in Sicily, rich in flocks,
> reaping the crested heads of every excellence.
> There his fame is magnified
> in the splendour of music, where
> we delight at the friendly table. Then take the Dorian lyre from its peg,
> if any glory of Pisa or Pherenikos
> slide with delight beneath your heart,
> when by Alpheus waters he sped
> his bulk, with the lash laid never on,
> and mixed in the arms of victory his lord,
>
> king of Syracuse, delighting in horses; and his fame shines
> among strong men where Lydian Pelops went to dwell . . . .

116

The hospitality lauded by Pindar was indeed on a grand scale: Gellias, one of the city's richest citizens, is said to have stationed servants before his gates with orders to invite every stranger to be his guest. When five hundred cavalry from Gela arrived soaked and chilled during a wintry storm, Gellias entertained them all, "and provided them all forthwith from his own stores with outer and under garments." His wine-cellar, according to a narrator who visited Akragas as a soldier, contained "three hundred great casks hewn out of the very rock, each of them with a capacity of one hundred amphoras (900 gallons), and beside them was a wine-vat, plastered with stucco and with a capacity of one thousand amphoras, from which the wine flowed into the casks."

Diodorus gives an account of the night the wedding of Antisthenes' daughter lit up the sky; there was

. . . . a party to all the citizens in the courtyards where they all lived and more than eight hundred chariots followed the bride in the procession; furthermore, not only the men on horseback from the city itself but also many from neighbouring cities who had been invited to the wedding joined to form the escort of the bride. But most extraordinary of all, we are told, was the provision for the lighting: the altars in all the temples and those in the courtyards throughout the city he had piled high with wood, and to the shopkeepers he gave firewood and brush with orders that when a fire was kindled on the acropolis they should all do the same; and when they did as they were ordered, at the time when the bride was brought to her home, since there were many torch-bearers in the procession, the city was filled with light, and the main streets through which the procession was to pass could not contain the accompanying throng, all the inhabitants zealously emulating the man's grand manner.

117

One of the city's own philosophers commented that the Akragantines "built their houses as though they were to live forever, but gave themselves to luxury as if they were to die tomorrow."

The Valley of Temples to the southeast of the city is in scale with this adage. Walking over to it from the residential area, with an almond orchard in fragrant flower on my right, my first distant view was of the Temple of Hera, high up at the extreme eastern end of the sacred precinct. Built between 460 and 440, the temple exemplifies the classical plan, with six columns on the ends, thirteen on the sides, a pronaos, cella, opisthodomos; traces of stairs indicate upper galleries like those at Paestum. Above the bloom, its terrace offered an overview of the entire ridge and the walls guarding it; to the south, the land slopes off steeply in cultivated fields, then rises again between the temples and the sea.

An early temple to Demeter is around the hill to the northeast, but a westerly view from the Temple of Hera takes in almost all of the other major shrines. As one walks towards the next in the series, Byzantine tombs line the way, cut into the city wall. Their presence would be more inappropriate if the interior of the temple known as the 'Concordia' because of an irrelevant Roman inscription had not been remodelled in the sixth century A.D. to serve as a Christian church.

Its appearance is distorted by the arches cut in the cella walls, but the exterior is well preserved: the peristyle and pediments are intact, and the impression given is very like that of the 'Concordia's' exact contemporary, the Hephaisteion in Athens, which likewise owes its good state of preservation to its early conversion from a pagan temple to a Christian sanctuary.

Beyond the 'Concordia' a villa surrounded by a garden houses photographs, models, records of excavations. It was built by an

Englishman, Captain Alexander Hardcastle, who, exiled to Sicily

for his health early in this century, became engrossed in the excavation and preservation of the temples and contributed time and funds to the work until his death in 1932.

At the west end of the garden, more flowering almonds frame a row of eight re-erected columns from the south side of the Temple of Herakles. Built at the end of the sixth century, this was the most archaic in style of the temple group, long and narrow, with six columns at the ends and fifteen at the sides.

The now-retired first custodian of the precinct, Antonio Arancio, who worked with Hardcastle, still spends hours there on busman's holiday. Under his guidance I saw details of the huge edifice of exceptional design erected by the Akragantines in honor of Olympian Zeus.

In all the Greek world, only four other temples approach its pretentiousness. There is the largest of the temples at Selinunte. There are two Hellenistic structures in Asia Minor, the Artemiseion at Ephesus and the Didymaeion at Miletus. There is the Olympeion at Athens. The last was modestly begun under Peisistratos; abandoned for four centuries to be resumed in the grand manner by a Syrian Grecophile in the second century B.C.; again abandoned; and completed in Corinthian profusion after another several centuries' delay under the Roman Emperor Hadrian, who added his own statue to the shrine of Zeus and came to Athens for the dedication. The Athenian Olympeion has 5,192 square feet of stylobate and columns fifty-six and a half feet high; that at Akragas, begun under Theron in 480 and ready for its roof seventy-four years later, when the Carthaginians overwhelmed the city, was slightly bigger still. At the altar in front of this temple, 480 oxen could be simultaneously sacrificed.

Many details of the Akragantine Olympeion's earthquake-riven architecture are uncertain, but the most unusual feature of its   *121* design is clear. Instead of a peristyle, it had walls at its outside edges strengthened by half-columns on the exterior and pilasters within. In some portion of the structure, perhaps on ledges more than halfway up these walls, giant telemons—male counterparts of the karyatids of the Erechtheion of Athens—stood with upraised arms and hands locked behind their heads, Atlas-like upholding the entablature.

The entranceways to admit worshippers may have been to right and left of the corner columns; since there were seven columns across the ends, there could have been no central portal.

The roof-plan of this building is one of its uncertainties: attempted spanning of so wide a space seems improbable. The roof may have been intended to cover the aisles only, leaving an hypaethral center open to the sky.

Of this temple Diodorus writes:

> Now the sacred buildings which they constructed, and especially the temple of Zeus, bear witness to the grand manner of the men of that day. Of the other sacred buildings some have been burned and others completely destroyed because of the many times the city has been taken in war, but the completion of the temple of Zeus, which was ready to receive its roof, was prevented by the war; and after the war, since the city had been completely destroyed, never in the subsequent years did the Acragantini find themselves able to finish their buildings. The temple has a length of three hundred and forty feet, a width of sixty, and a height of one hundred and twenty not including the foundation. And being as it is the largest temple in Sicily, it may not unreasonably be compared, so far as the magnitude of its substructure is concerned, with the temples outside of Sicily; for even though, as it turned out, the design could not be carried out, the scale of the undertaking at any rate is clear. And though all other men build their

temples either with walls forming the sides or with rows of columns, thus enclosing their sanctuaries, this temple combines both these plans; for the columns were built in with the walls, the part extending outside the temple being rounded and that within square; and the circumference of the outer part of the column which extends from the wall is twenty feet and the body of a man may be contained in the fluting, while that of the inner part is twelve feet. The porticoes were of enormous size and height, and in the east pediment they portrayed The Battle between the Gods and the Giants in sculptures which excelled in size and beauty, and in the west The Capture of Troy, in which each one of the heroes may be seen portrayed in a manner appropriate to his role.

Mr. Arancio led me to a fluted drum-fragment, around which the leaves of an acanthus plant grew as if to supply it with a Corinthian capital. The literary exaggeration about the columns

persisted from Diodorus to Goethe—in his *Italian Journey* the German Romantic wrote:

> The only recognizable shapes in all this heap of rubble are a triglyph and half of a column, both of gigantic proportions. I tried to measure the triglyph with my outstretched arms and found I could not span it. As for the column, this will give you some idea of its size. When I stood in one of the flutings as in a niche, my shoulders barely touched both edges. It would take twenty-two men, placed shoulder to shoulder, to form a circle approximating in size to the circumference of such a column.

But they are still huge.

He indicated other fragments that showed the polycentric shaping which gave the columns perspective: along the rows, the drums were expanded slightly outward, and the corner ones expanded in two directions to match the lines converging on them from left and right.

The column-sections were trundled onto the site; he exhibited a drawing of how axles, blocked at their outer ends and passed through rollers, were driven into the flat sides of the drums.

The plinths of the entablature were hauled up into place by pulleys; U-shaped grooves, carved into their butt ends, slotted the ropes firmly into place. Some of the heaviest blocks have two U-s, slightly inclined toward each other to equalize the stress.

He displayed the temple's massive substructure—on the south side, we looked down foundation walls eighteen feet deep.

As he talked, I could imagine the noise and shouting of hundreds of sweating men.

One of the telemons—there are fragments of others—has been reassembled; with his twenty-five and a half foot length stretched on the ground, he flexes his biceps as he lies. Diodorus' statement that the east pediment of this Gargantuan edifice was decorated with a Battle of the Giants seems wholly appropriate, though other evidence is lacking.

125

Mr. Arancio's dedication to things Greek determined him to name his son and daughter Ulysses and Penelope. With relish, he recounted how the Catholic priest of their parish told the children's church-going mother that these were pagan names, unsuitable for Christian baptism; for the girl, he suggested, perhaps Helena? Via his wife, Mr. Arancio replied that the original baptism in the River Jordan had been an informal affair, and that if the priest did not care to baptize his children with the names he chose he could take a little water and do it himself. As to Helena, he would point out that it was the name of the pagan Helen of Troy, who moreover was a very bad wife, whereas Penelope was a paragon, willing to wait for her husband twenty years.

Beyond the Temple of Zeus, passing a number of small uncolumned shrines to minor earth deities, some with circular altars, I approached an archaeological embarrassment. The picturesque ruin—four columns and an entablature like the corner of a temple—known as the Temple of the Dioskouri is familiar in many lands from travel posters advertising Sicily. But the fragments of which it is composed are of different dates and from different buildings. The pieces were put together in the nineteenth century. The undecided question: to let be, or not to be?

Yet in one particular this structure helps convey an idea of the appearance of Greek temples built of limestone in their great days: some of its columns and stones retain fragments of the white plaster which gave such buildings the appearance of marble. The fifth-century traveller approaching Akragas from the sea looked up the sweep of fields, green in springtime, fair with the bent crested heads of ripe wheat in June, tawny under the summer sun, to a ridge crowned with white shrines, here and there picked out in brilliant color.

126   Past the Dioskouri, more small temples, and a larger one that

may have been to Demeter and Kore, the land slants steeply downwards. Further around the hill, out of sight, two fluted columns of a Temple of Hephaistos display an Ionic influence rare in Sicily.

Near the junction of the city's two rivers, a temple of Askleipios, built in the second half of the fifth century, had half-columns on its west end similar, in miniature, to those of the temple of Zeus.

The city museum exhibits both polychrome terra cotta decorations from the temple of Hephaistos and lion water spouts from an early temple to Demeter and Kore now incorporated in the Church of San Biagio. (Another early shrine, perhaps to Athena, lies beneath the church of Santa Maria dei Greci; on the acropolis, San Gerlando rises above the temple of Zeus.)

127

The Magnificent Tyrants

Unlike the mayor's office at Castelvetrano, this museum has succeeded in retaining its fifth-century kouros, a marble of Theron's time. An extensive series of vases, both red-figured and white-backgrounded, displays exquisitely drawn scenes; one fragment of a huge vase rim presents a spirited battle between Greeks and centaurs. Among the terra cotta heads is an exceptional Athena. A Hellenistic relief shows a winged Eros and Psyche flying upward above curling waves; their parallel rising curves are like the flight of whistling swans. There are many vivacious figurines, together with the moulds for making them.

Yet in view of the magnificent art objects that were once in Akragas, the present collections seem skimpy. The statue of Apollo for the temple of Asklepios was the work of the sculptor Myron. Zeuxis of Heraclea in southern Italy, whose paintings were so lifelike that his grapes deceived the birds, is known to have painted for Akragas both Alkmene, the mother of Herakles, and a scene showing her infant son strangling the snakes that menaced him in his cradle. The latter was in the temple of Herakles.

While musing on the spoliation and destruction that robbed Akragas and succeeding generations of its treasures, I took grim satisfaction in the failure of one such effort, reported by Cicero:

> . . . . not far from the market-place of Agrigentum there is a temple of Hercules which they regard with much awe and reverence. In this temple there is a bronze image of Hercules himself . . . . it is so lovely, gentlemen, that its mouth and chin are quite noticeably rubbed from the way in which people, when praying or offering thanks, not only do reverence to it but actually kiss it. A body of armed slaves, led by Timarchides, suddenly descended upon this temple late one night when Verres was staying in the town. The watchmen and temple guards raised the alarm, and at first did their best to resist and repel the attack, but

were savagely knocked about with clubs and cudgels, and in the end beaten off. Then the bolts were wrenched off and the doors broken open, and they tried to loosen the statue and lever it off its pedestal with crowbars. Meanwhile the shouts of alarm had informed the whole town that an assault was being made on their ancestral gods: no unforeseen invasion by an enemy or surprise attack by pirates—a company of armed and equipped gaol-birds taken from the governor's staff had come there from the governor's house. There was not a man in Agrigentum that night so old or infirm that he did not get out of his bed, when this news aroused him, and lay hold of the first weapon that came to hand; so that in a short time there was a rush to the temple from all parts of the town. Already for more than an hour a crowd of fellows had been trying hard to get the statue off its pedestal, without its coming loose anywhere for all their efforts, though some tried to lever it up from below, and others to drag it forward with ropes tied to its arms and legs. Then suddenly the townsfolk in a body went for them with a great shower of stones, and the nocturnal troops of our eminent commander took to their heels and fled. However, they carried off a couple of small statuettes, so as not to report back to this sacrilegious pirate quite empty-handed. Sicilians are always ready with some appropriate jest, even under the most trying circumstances; thus on the present occasion they observed that this monstrous hog ought to be counted among the labours of Hercules quite as much as the celebrated Erymanthian boar.

What does remain of the great art of Akragas in some profusion is its coinage. One symbol of the city was the crab. It is superbly presented, whether alone, with vigilant protruding eyes and toothed foreclaws open for a pinch, as in the early issues, or accompanied by a spine-tailed sea monster, perhaps Scylla herself, looping through the water with Hellenistic abandon.

Still more splendid are the eagles of Akragas. Earlier coins   *129* show one bird attacking a snake. At the height of the great period, a pair of eagles dismember a hare. One, wings folded, lifts his beak to swallow. The other, wings upraised, bends toward his prey.

This was Zeus's bird. Bacchylides, who visited the courts of the magnificent tyrants, exalted the strength and sovereignty alike of the eagle and of his patron in that part of his poem, *The Eagle of Song*, that reads:

> *Across the sky through gulfs profound*
> > *Great strength conveys him undismayed,*
> *While smaller fowl with piping sound*
> > *Shrink back to earth afraid.*
> *No peak that the giant earth upheaves,*
> > *No rough sea-wave unwearying*
> *Can stay him: the fathomless air he cleaves*
> > *And so will veer and lean his wing*
> *To the west wind's breath as he sails in sight*
> > *On plume of delicate pencilling*
> > > *That every eye*
> > > *Must testify*
> > *The bird of sovran flight.*
> *By thousand ways I too may sail*
> > *And praise of Hiero's house declare*
> *While Arês goes in coat of mail*
> > *And Victory shakes her raven hair.*

CHAPTER VIII

The Western Defense

Not only in Akragas but in most of the Sicilian and South Italian city-states, one-man rule was a repeated pattern. Constitutional governments, with elections by some or all of the citizens, existed intermittently: famous law-codes included the early seventh century aristocratic constitution drawn up by Zaleucus at the time of the founding of the Lokrians' South Italian settlement, which both Pindar and Demosthenes regarded as a model; and that of Diocles of Syracuse at the end of the fifth century.

But military necessity, desire for conquest, and internal power-plays continued to bring dictatorship back again.

Then, the word tyrant did not carry the pejorative meaning it conveys today. Tyrants seized and held their power by force, exercised it subject to no restraint, and perpetrated notorious cruelties. But many of them were great generals who fought wide-sweeping wars, lavish patrons of the arts, public figures who brought their cities riches and renown.

The times combined civilization and savagery. The accepted consequence of defeat in war was torture, mass slaughter, removal or sale into slavery of entire populations. Ovid's *Tristia* tells of Phalaris, a mid-sixth century tyrant of Akragas, to whom Busiris brought a specially-designed instrument of torture:

> And gave the bull, they say, to the Sicilian lord commending his work of art with the words: 'In this gift, O King, there is profit, greater than appears, for not the appearance alone of my work is worthy of praise. Seest thou on the right that the bull's flank may be opened? Through this thou must thrust whomsoever thou wouldst destroy. Forthwith shut him in and roast him over slow-burning coals: he will bellow, and that will be the voice of a true bull. For this invention pay gift with gift, and give me, I pray thee, a reward worthy of my genius.' Thus he spake. But Phalaris said, 'Marvellous inventor of punishment, dedicate in person thine own work!' At once roasted by the fires to which he had himself cruelly pointed the way he uttered with groaning lips sounds twofold.

But Phalaris is said to have made further use of the bull thereafter.

Dionysius I of Syracuse, when his courtier Damocles waxed lyrical about the life of a tyrant, suspended a sword by a hair and bade him sit under it at a banquet and make merry. When the poet Philoxenus criticized his poems, Dionysius condemned him 132 to the stone quarries.

On the other hand, Cicero tells how this same tyrant was touched by the friendship of the Pythagoreans Damon and Phintias:

> They say that Damon and Phintias, of the Pythagorean school, enjoyed such ideally perfect friendship, that when the tyrant Dionysius had appointed a day for the execution of one of them, and the one who had been condemned to death requested a few days' respite for the purpose of putting his loved ones in the care of friends, the other became surety for his appearance, with the understanding that if his friend did not return, he himself should be put to death. And when the friend returned on the day appointed, the tyrant in admiration for their faithfulness begged that they would enrol him as a third partner in their friendship.

The tyrant who consolidated southeast Sicily and made Syracuse the island's center of power and culture was Gelon of Gela, the next city east of Agrigento on the south coast some sixty crow-flight miles west of Syracuse. He had been chief of cavalry to his city's preceding tyrant, Hippocrates, who had waged successful and well-requited war on Syracuse but not followed up his victory with occupation. Gelon set aside Hippocrates' sons, quelled an uprising in Gela, connived with displaced Syracusan aristocrats—he is alleged to have said, "the common people is a most thankless housemate"—and obtained Syracuse without a struggle in 485.

By a symbolic chance, the classical remains most prominent in Gelon's native city are monuments to the art of war. These are the tremendous walls along the dunes of Capo Soprano northwest of the city. Again and again, from the days of the Carthaginians to those of the Allies of World War II, the coast from this point west has been the landing spot of seaborne armies from Africa. Recent removal of tons of sand has revealed defenses up to twenty-

five feet high. The tallest are now enclosed in plexiglass and roofed over to preserve late additions of top courses made of mud-brick; the lower courses are of well-fitted stone. These walls, built by Timoleon of Syracuse, date only from the latter half of the fourth century, but they memorialize the force by which Gelon of Gela gave Syracuse its early primacy.

Such remains of the ancient city as were not destroyed by the Carthaginians in the third century lie directly under the modern town—a single re-erected column in a park at its eastern end and some newly excavated houses nearby are all that can be seen.

Even the superb horse's head in the Museum, part of an akroterion, was dredged up from the bottom of the Museum's well.

The city boasted an exceptionally fine pottery industry—its
vases are displayed from Palermo to Syracuse as well as in the
Gela Museum, where many terra cotta Gorgon's faces, cross-eyed
and tongue-protruding, and Sileni, bald of head, bulbous of nose
and equine of ears, grimace from the shelves.

On most of the city's coinage, a fierce bull with the face of a man represents the rampaging river from which Gela took its name; another design is that of a horseman. Gelon the tyrant drew qualities from both.

Leaving his brother Hieron to govern Gela, Gelon moved to Syracuse, started naval construction, strengthened fortifications. He sold many of the democratically-minded Syracusan citizens into slavery, transplanting large populations from nearby southeastern cities to replace them; established a mercenary army with the island of Ortygia as its citadel; and expanded the city along the adjacent bays. From his day, Syracuse was undefeated for three hundred years.

His father-in-law Theron, in conquering new territory for Akragas, induced a major war. About 483 he thrust across the island and captured Himera on the north coast. The expelled tyrant, Terrilus, fled to the protection of his son-in-law, Anaxilas, who controlled Messana and Rhegium. Already allied to Carthage, these two appealed for North African help.

For three years, both sides built strength.

Simultaneously, a comparably decisive contest was preparing between Persia and mainland Greece. In 490, Darius had been repelled at Marathon. His son Xerxes was about to try again.

Envoys from Athens and Sparta, for once acting in concert, came to Gelon, warning him that if the Persians overran the Greek peninsula, Sicily would be their next objective. Herodotus recounts their appeal for men and ships:

> For if all Greece join together in one, there will be a mighty host collected, and we shall be a match for our assailants; but if some turn traitors, and others refuse their aid, and only a small part of the whole body remains sound, then there is reason to fear

that all Greece may perish. For do not thou cherish a hope that the Persian, when he has conquered our country, will be content and not advance against thee. . . .

Gelon, recalling previous denial of help when he had been the suppliant, replied:

But though ye slighted me then, I will not imitate you now: I am ready to give you aid, and to furnish as my contribution two hundred triremes, twenty thousand men-at-arms, two thousand cavalry, and an equal number of archers, slingers, and light horse-men, together with corn for the whole Grecian army so long as the war shall last. These services, however, I promise on one condition—that ye appoint me chief captain and commander of the Grecian forces during the war with the barbarian. Unless ye agree to this, I will neither send succours, nor come myself.

His arrogance outraged the Spartan envoy:

Surely a groan would burst from Pelops' son, Agamemnon, did he hear that her leadership was snatched from Sparta by Gelo and the men of Syracuse. Speak then no more of any such condition, as that we should yield thee the chief command; but if thou art minded to come to the aid of Greece, prepare to serve under Lacedaemonian generals.

The Athenian envoy terminated the interview:

King of the Syracusans! Greece sent us here to thee to ask for an army, and not to ask for a general.

And so no Syracusan forces appeared at Thermopylae or Sala-mis.

Because they stayed at home, they were ready to meet the Carthaginians at Himera.

Herodotus' figure of 300,000 men strains modern credulity, but Carthage had assembled a very mighty force with invasion of Sicily in view. It was commanded by Hamilcar, son of its King Hannon and a Syracusan mother. In a move synchronized with Xerxes'—Phoenician ships fought at both Salamis and Himera—Hamilcar concentrated his land and sea forces at Panormus (Palermo), the easternmost harbor in Punic territory on the north coast, intending to join Terillus and Anaxilas at the Straits and then drive south to Syracuse. Gelon and Theron decided on an overland march across the center of the island, to attack Hamilcar as he moved east.

Desiring to open his campaign with suitable sacrifice to the Greek Poseidon, Hamilcar, from his camp at Himera, had sent to his Greek allies in the south, the Selinuntines, for information about proper ritual. By impersonating their momentarily expected envoys, Gelon and his men gained unchallenged entry into the Himeran camp.

The result was a total rout. Hamilcar, when he saw the magnitude of the disaster, immolated himself by jumping into the flames on the altar. The entire Carthaginian army surrendered; the fleet was destroyed. Diodorus says that "only a few survivors in one small boat reached home to give the brief news that all who crossed over to Sicily had perished."

The battles of Himera and Salamis were fought the same year—tradition fondly sets them on the same day. The defeat of the Persians was so decisive that they did not try again. The repulse of the Carthaginians was not final but gave a respite from war. Neither the Greek city-states of the Greek peninsula nor those in the west were overrun as the Greek city-states of Asia Minor had been in the previous century. Both remained free to develop their own institutions and history.

Most of the Carthaginians were enslaved. In addition, Carthage paid a heavy indemnity. But their penalty for failure could have been heavier. Because Hamilcar's mother was a Syracusan, Demarete, Theron's daughter and Gelon's wife, interceded for the vanquished. Gelon and Theron did not press their advantage, either in Sicily or in North Africa.

The grateful Carthaginians made Demarete a magnificent gift from which were minted commemorative silver coins called Demareteia in her honor. These ten-drachma pieces show a head of Artemis-Arethusa surrounded by dolphins on the obverse; the reverse displays a slow quadriga with Nike flying above to crown the charioteer; a small lion, symbolic of North Africa, is in the exergue below the horses' feet. In size and workmanship these coins excelled in a region of superb coinage.

Major votives expressed the Greeks' rejoicing. Themistocles began the renewal of Athens that Pericles consummated. At the same time Gelon and Theron erected an imposing temple at Himera. Close to the shore, on the very edge of Punic territory,

in plain sight of Solus (Solunte) and the eastern headland of Palermo's harbor, it was a monument to victory in the teeth of the Carthaginians. On its coins, a cock crows.

Gold robed its statue to Zeus—a later tyrant who removed the precious metal excused himself on the ground that it was too heavy for the god in summer and too cold in winter, whereas wool would be suitable to both. Gold, fifty talents worth, was likewise lavished on the Deinomenid votive at Delphi: four round bases, which still exist, one for each of the brothers, supported tripods and a golden Victory. Bacchylides in his third ode memorializes the "high shining tripods which glowed in front of the temple." At Akragas, Theron put his captives to work on the Olympeion. At Syracuse, Gelon erected a new temple to Athena.

Throughout Syracusan history, the city's life focused on the island of Ortygia. A short bridge connects island and mainland. The Little Harbor, protected by breakwaters, lies to the north.

The Great Harbor circles to the south with an enclosing peninsula which curves so far towards Ortygia's eastern tip that the passage to and from the open sea is narrow.

The island's name is the early name of Cycladic Delos, where Artemis was born; while she liked to hunt in central Sicily, her chief Sicilian shrine was here.

The woman's head on Syracusan coins is either hers or that of the nymph Arethusa, to whom was sacred a freshwater spring on the island close by the sea.

Ancient sources explain the origin of its fresh water by recounting that when Arethusa lived at her home in western Greece she was desired by the god of the River Alpheus that flows through the Peloponnese beside the site of the Olympic Games. To escape him, she turned herself into a river and plunged westward into the Ionian Sea, coming to the surface at Syracuse. Alpheus gave hot pursuit and appeared offshore, bubbling up through the salt water. Pausanias declares

> that the river flows over the sea and there mingles its water with the spring I cannot choose but believe, knowing as I do that the god at Delphi countenances the story; for when he was sending Archias the Corinthian to found Syracuse, he uttered these verses also:

> *There lies an isle, Ortygia, in the dim sea*
> *Off Trinacria, where Alpheus's mouth bubbles*
> *As it mingles with the springs of the fair-flowing Arethusa.*

The geographer Strabo records that

> a certain cup, they think, was thrown out into the river at Olympia and was discharged into the fountain; and again, the fountain was discoloured as a result of sacrifices of oxen at Olympia.

From the earliest days, an image of Olympian Hera on the tip
of Ortygia was a landmark for sailors; crews putting out carried
with them ashes that they poured into the sea when they could
no longer discern the statue. A sixth-century temple to Apollo, on
the island, and, south of the city on the shore of the Great Harbor,
the remains of an early Olympeion to Zeus can still be seen.

Likewise on the island was a precinct from the archaic period
dedicated to Athena. Parts of its painted terra cotta entablature
are in the Syracuse Museum—on a rainy day, the extended pipe-
like downspouts that disposed of the water from its roof must have
created an aerial fountain. From the center of the tympanum, a
full-figured, winged Gorgon holding a small horse is as vividly
colored as if painted yesterday.

142   Gelon replaced this temple with a Doric design in stone. The

pillars of its peristyle can still be seen in the outside north wall of the church—the present cathedral—into which the building was converted in the seventh century A.D., and along both north and south walls within. Inner columns of the former shrine, together with square pillars cut from the walls of the old cella, now set off the narthex and the aisles of the church nave.

Adornment of Syracuse continued after Gelon's death in 478 when Hieron came from Gela to replace him. He likewise maintained Gelon's other policies. To the north, he forcibly ejected the Ionian population of Catana, bringing in new settlers as more reliable allies and naming his new town Aetna. With the Cumaeans, he repelled an outside threat to the Greek communities by victory in a sea-fight with the Etruscans in 474; he commemorated the event with a votive monument at Delphi as well as the helmet at Olympia.

As an art patron, Hieron entertained at his court both Pindar and the two poets, Simonides and his nephew Bacchylides, whom Pindar openly disdained as inferior competitors. He built Syracuse's first stone theater.

The Athenian tragedian Aeschylus made at least three visits to the city, the first two in Hieron's time. About 476 the tyrant commissioned him to write and produce a play about his new foundation to the north—of the script of *The Aetnaeans* only fragments now remain.

After staging his *Persians* in Athens in 472, Aeschylus returned to Sicily to give a repeat performance at Syracuse. While the script recounts the defeat of Xerxes, it portrays the war with great compassion, and from the standpoint of the vanquished. The acclaim given to this play in both cities, so soon after Salamis and Himera, contrasts with the cruelty exercised at the time of both triumphs. The author had himself fought at Marathon.

Aeschylus went to Sicily for the third time after presentation of his *Oresteia* in Athens in 458. Two years later he died and was buried at Gela. What may be a legendary account of the manner of his death is given in the *Life of Aeschylus* preserved in a Florentine manuscript of the eleventh century A.D. The dramatist had long been wholly bald: his head had the look of weathered marble. Seagulls or birds of prey, when they find clams or tortoises, drop them from heights on hard surfaces to crack the shells. An eagle with a tortoise mistook the head of Aeschylus.

Pausanias, when describing Greek pride in the battle of Marathon, says of the epitaph carved on his tomb: "Even Aeschylus, in the prospect of death, though his reputation as a poet stood so high . . . recorded nothing but his father's name, and his own name, and his city, and that the grove at Marathon and the Medes who landed in it were the witnesses of his manhood."

Theron died in 472 and Hieron in 466; each was succeeded by a relative against whom the people rebelled. Democratic governments were instituted in Akragas and Syracuse.

Over the next few decades the cultural life of the region was enriched by men who had been born in Sicily. Gorgias of Leontini, the developer of rhetoric, repaid part of Sicily's earlier cultural debt to Athens: towards the end of the fifth century, he settled in Greece for the rest of his life, teaching rhetoric and oratory. Plato made him and his young pupil Polus the central figures of his dialogue, *Gorgias*, in which Socrates confutes the pupil's defense of tyranny and Gorgias exalts the power of words while disclaiming responsibility on the part of those who teach men to use them for what such men may subsequently do with their power.

Gorgias' own tutor was the most learned and certainly the most colorful of mid-fifth century citizens of Akragas: Empedocles— 144 philosopher, doctor, orator, poet, and democrat.

His belief in popular government made him instrumental in throwing out the oligarchy that followed the Emmenidae, and he firmly refused the urgent invitation of his fellow-citizens to become their king.

His system of philosophy posited four elements—earth, air, water, fire; he believed that combinations of these, induced by the antithetical forces of love and hate, constitute all forms of animate and inanimate life. Since he held the less viable combinations to disappear, and the more viable to continue, his system affords an early parallel to Darwin's *Origin of Species*.

He wrote two major poems, *On Nature* and *Purifications*, but they exist only in fragmentary form. He apparently shared Pythagoras' belief in the transmigration of souls.

Even in his life-time Empedocles was a charismatic figure: Diodorus describes him as laurel-wreathed, robed like a god in purple, sandalled in gold. He taught that the highest forms of human life, the closest to the divine, were the prophet and the physician. He was both. As a living myth, he attracted legend. Most spectacular of unsupported tales is the account of his death by suicidal leap into Aetna's crater: self-immolation in the expectation of becoming, or at least being worshipped as a god. The mountain, it is said, later gave back one golden sandal.

CHAPTER IX

View from Euryalus

On a spring day of utter clarity, high wind chased white clouds across a sky the color of the white-capped sea. It whipped my topcoat against my legs. A copy of Thucydides in my pocket, high on the formidable walls of Fort Euryalus, I surveyed the landscape around Syracuse.

To Syracuse, as to Athens, the mid-fifth century had afforded a respite from history.

One brief though serious threat followed establishment of a cohesive Sikel state by the native general Ducetius, who rallied his people in the mountains between Gela and Aetna, won impor- *147* tant victories and set up a capital, but was defeated and banished to Corinth.

During these years, the southeast of the island became a Dorian granary—wheat poured east to Corinth and Sparta, supplying these centers over a route both shorter and safer than that traversed by the grain fleet the Athenians sent every autumn to the far shores of the Black Sea.

At the same time, ships were getting larger and faster. In the early city states, population pressure had had to be met by emigration; now, better communications offered the possibility of maintaining larger numbers at home, if sources and supply routes could be kept under reliable control. The next phase in history was foreseeable: larger political structures governing wider-spread territories would take shape.

Athens began to look toward Sicily.

The league formed after Salamis, through which Aegean island allies paid tribute to Athens in return for protection, was shaken when Pericles impounded the treasury at Delos and used the money to build the new Athenian acropolis. It had been based on common military danger; as the danger receded, its cohesiveness wore thin. Athens sought new alliances with an eye to economic as well as military strength. The greatest concentration of economic strength was in the territory controlled by Syracuse.

Ionian colonies such as Leontini to the north of Syracuse and Rhegium at the Straits were already in alliance with Athens—it was with a delegation from Leontini seeking Athenian support that Gorgias first came to Greece. During the mid-'50's, Athens made a treaty with Segesta—its text still exists. In 434, war broke out between Corinth and her ancient island colony of Korkyra (Corfu), now a powerful maritime rival. The Korkyrans appealed to Athens, whose fleet arrived just in time to join an already-en-

148

gaged naval battle and tip the balance. Henceforth, the island that had long guarded the sea route to the west for the Dorians was an Ionian ally. The Corinthians took their grievance to Sparta; the first phase of the Peloponnesian War ensued.

In 429 plague raged in Athens, and Pericles died of it. After his death the Athenians diverted strength to intervene in Sicilian quarrels. Thucydides reveals their undeclared aspiration:

> They virtuously professed that they were going to assist their own kinsmen and their newly-acquired allies, but the simple truth was that they aspired to the empire of Sicily.

Some Athenian leaders were even thinking in terms of Sicily today, tomorrow North Africa—the most active proponent of the larger scheme was named Hyperbolus. Sensing the change, Hermocrates of Syracuse convened a conference of Sicilian city states at Gela that declared a doctrine of Sicily for the Sicilians.

Meanwhile the Segestaeans had attacked the Selinuntines, who summoned Syracusan aid. As Segesta became hard-pressed, envoys went to Athens to ask help under their alliance, even offering to bear the cost of the war.

The Athenians cannily sent to see if the Segestaean store of treasure was really as massive as described. These emissaries were duped. According to Thucydides,

> The fact was that when the original envoys came from Athens to inspect the treasure, the Egestaeans had practiced a trick upon them. They brought them to the temple of Aphroditè at Eryx, and showed them the offerings deposited there, consisting of bowls, flagons, censers, and a good deal of other plate. Most of the vessels were only of silver, and therefore they made a show quite out of proportion to their value. They also gave private entertainments to

the crews of the triremes: on each of these occasions they produced, as their own, drinking-vessels of gold and silver not only collected in Egesta itself, but borrowed from the neighbouring towns, Phoenician as well as Hellenic. All of them exhibiting much the same vessels and making everywhere a great display, the sailors were amazed, and on their arrival in Athens told every one what heaps of wealth they had seen.

The returning heralds bore twice thirty talents of silver. The Athenian Assembly voted an expedition. Its actual aim was the capture of Syracuse.

Close to the sea north of Syracuse, a steep-sided ridge called the Epipolae rises abruptly, runs west for some four miles, breaks, and resumes again. Fort Euryalus stands at the break. From its upper levels, the entire terrain of the Athenian-Syracusan struggle is in view.

Southeast lies the city: the island of Ortygia, city center from the beginning; Achradina, its first mainland extension across the narrow dividing channel; the periphery of further settlement along the foot of the Epipolae—Tyche, the temple area of Apollo Temenites and the theater, Neapolis.

Between these settlements and the Fort the cross-walls thrown up in competitive haste by the opposing armies made circuits over the Epipolae.

Buildings hide the Little Harbor to the north of Ortygia, but not the Great Harbor to the south. Midway along its shore, near the Olympeion, the swamp-surrounded river Anapus flows into the bay; then the curve sweeps upward to the point of Plemmyrium, opposite Ortygia's fortified tip.

On the coast to the north of the city, past green fields, the slender peninsula of Thapsos projects into the sea. Out of view past the

next peninsula, the site of Leontini lay in the near foothills and
Catana across the river in the plain.

Taking shelter high on an east-facing rampart, I opened my
Thucydides at the sixth book, and re-read the entire story.

Thucydides was an Athenian, but his balanced fairness makes
less disappointing the disappearance of the equally contemporary
version of this struggle written by the Syracusan Philistus, whose
History has come down only in transmitted quotes. Thucydides'
text reflects his extraordinary opportunities for firsthand observa-
tion of both sides. He was present during the events in Athens that
preceded the decision to undertake the Syracusan war. Because *151*

his family had holdings—gold mines—in Thrace, he was named one of two generals to go there and defend the Athenian outposts essential to protection of the Dardanelles grain route. He failed. In 423, the Spartan general Brasidas captured Athens' main Thracian settlement. The Assembly exiled Thucydides.

With his exile as a passport, he visited the Peloponnese. After the end of hostilities, he went to Syracuse, saw the topography, questioned Athenian prisoners. The terse, epic quality of his writing gives to the tragedy enacted within sight of Euryalus dimensions similar to those of the encounter before the walls of Troy.

On a late June day of 415, all Athens flocked to the Peiraeus to watch the sails lift on a hundred ships:

> On the fleet the greatest pains and expense had been lavished by the trierarchs and the state. The public treasury gave a drachma a day to each sailor, and furnished empty hulls for sixty swift-sailing vessels, and for forty transports carrying hoplites, all these were manned with the best crews which could be obtained. The trierarchs, besides the pay given by the state, added somewhat more out of their own means to the wages of the upper ranks of rowers and of the petty officers. The figureheads and other fittings provided by them were of the most costly description. Everyone strove to the utmost that his own ship might excel both in beauty and swiftness. The infantry had been well selected and the lists carefully made up. There was the keenest rivalry among the soldiers in the matter of arms and personal equipment . . . . . Never had a greater expedition been sent to a foreign land; never was there an enterprise in which the hope of future success seemed to be better justified by actual power.
>
> When the ships were manned and everything required for the voyage had been placed on board, silence was proclaimed by the sound of the trumpet, and all with one voice before setting sail offered up the customary prayers; these were recited, not in each

ship, but by a single herald, the whole fleet accompanying him. On every deck both officers and men, mingling wine in bowls, made libations from vessels of gold and silver. The multitude of citizens and other well-wishers who were looking on from the land joined in the prayer. The crews raised the Paean and, when the libations were completed, put to sea. After sailing out for some distance in single file, the ships raced with one another as far as Aegina; thence they hastened onwards to Corcyra, where the allies who formed the rest of the army were assembling.

Two years later, both this fleet and the second force sent to its relief in 413 were gone. Few indeed of those who sailed ever came home again.

Like the intervention of the gods in the *Iliad,* the fortunes of war favored now this side, now that—with only small differences at critical moments, the outcome might have gone the other way. Yet it can be argued that the disaster did not occur at Syracuse; that it had already occurred at home before the expedition started; that it was implicit alike in the motives of the political decision by which the Athenians committed themselves to this aggression, and in the quality of the citizens whom the Assembly appointed to be generals.

Unresolved divisions as to policy were represented in a triple joint-command. There was the temperate Nicias, conservative aristocrat who on the death of Pericles was recognized as the city's ranking citizen, sensitive and sure in his feeling for history, mistaken and vacillating when the moment came to act. He disapproved of the expedition. He was named to go. He went.

There was the flashing Alcibiades, scion of the Alkmeionid family—Pericles' own—drunk with magnificence, personable, brilliant, voluble, treasonable, in debt.

And there was the soldier's soldier, Lamachus, who, impassive 153 and overruled in the hour when earth's foundations fled, found an early grave.

Thucydides' epic depicts the duel before the Athenian Assembly of Nicias and Alcibiades. Nicias said:

> I know that we are assembled here to discuss the preparations which are required for our expedition to Sicily, but in my judgment it is still a question whether we ought to go thither at all; we should not be hasty in determining a matter of so much importance, or allow ourselves to rush into an impolitic war at the instigation of foreigners. . . .

> I tell you that in going to Sicily you are leaving many enemies behind you, and seem to be bent on trying to bring new ones hither. You are perhaps relying upon the treaty recently made [with Sparta], which if you remain quiet may retain the name of a treaty; for to a mere name the intrigues of certain persons both here and at Lacedaemon have nearly succeeded in reducing it. . . . .

> The Chalcidians in Thrace have been rebels all these years and remain unsubdued, and there are other subjects of ours in various parts of the mainland who are uncertain in their allegiance. . . . The Hellenes in Sicily will dread us most if we never come; in a less degree if we display our strength and speedily depart; but if any disaster occur, they will despise us and be ready enough to join the enemies who are attacking us here. . . . There was a time when you feared the Lacedaemonians and their allies, but now you have got the better of them, and because your first fears have not been realized you despise them, and even hope to conquer Sicily. . . .

> We must remember also that we have only just recovered in some measure from a great plague and a great war, and are beginning to make up our losses in men and money. It is our duty to expend our

154

new resources upon ourselves at home, and not upon begging exiles who have an interest in successful lies. . . .

I dare say there may be some young man here who is delighted at holding a command, and the more so because he is too young for his post; and he, regarding only his own interest, may recommend you to sail; he may be one who is much admired for his stud of horses, and wants to make something out of his command which will maintain him in his extravagance. . . . The youth of whom I am speaking has summoned to his side young men like himself, whom, not without alarm, I see sitting by him. . . . Do not, like them, entertain a desperate craving for things out of your reach; you know that by prevision many successes are gained, but few or none by mere greed. On behalf of our country, now on the brink of the greatest danger which she has ever known, I entreat you to hold up your hands against them.

When he had finished Alcibiades spoke:

I have a better right to command, men of Athens, than another; for as Nicias has attacked me, I must begin by praising myself; and I consider that I am worthy. Those doings of mine for which I am so much cried out against are an honour to myself and to my ancestors, and a solid advantage to my country. In consequence of the distinguished manner in which I represented the state at Olympia, the other Hellenes formed an idea of our power which even exceeded the reality, although they had previously imagined that we were exhausted by war. I sent into the lists seven chariots,—no other private man ever did the like; I was victor, and also won the second and fourth prize; and I ordered everything in a style worthy of my victory.

The general sentiment honours such magnificence; and the energy which is shown by it creates an impression of power. . . . There is some use in the folly of a man who at his own cost benefits not only himself, but the state. . . . .

Did I not, without involving you in any great danger or expense, combine the most powerful states of Peloponnesus against the Lacedaemonians, whom I compelled to stake at Mantinea all that they had upon the fortune of one day? and even to this hour, though they were victorious in the battle, they have hardly recovered courage. . . . And now do not be afraid of me because I am young, but while I am in the flower of my days and Nicias enjoys the reputation of success, use the services of us both. Having determined to sail, do not change your minds under the impression that Sicily is a great power. . . .

Like all other imperial powers, we have acquired our dominion by our readiness to assist any one, whether Barbarian or Hellene, who may have invoked our aid. If we are all to sit and do nothing, or to draw distinctions of race when our help is requested, we shall add little to our empire, and run a great risk of losing it altogether. . . .

My opinion in short is, that a state used to activity will quickly be ruined by the change to inaction; and that they of all men enjoy the greatest security who are truest to themselves and their institutions even when they are not the best.

Seeing that Alcibiades had swayed the people, Nicias warned of the dangers of such an effort, projected the magnitude of preparation required. His estimates in no way disconcerted the Assembly: it voted to mount an enterprise of proportions unseen since the time of Xerxes.

In his *Acharnians,* Aristophanes describes the readying of troops on such a scale:

> *You would have launched at once three hundred gallies,*
> *And filled the city with the noise of troops;*

And crews of ships, crowding and clamouring
About the muster-masters and pay-masters;
With measuring corn out at the magazine,
And all the porch choked with the multitude;
With figures of Minerva, newly furbished,
Painted and gilt, parading in the streets;
With wineskins, kegs, and firkins, leeks and onions;
With garlic crammed in pouches, nets, and pokes;
With garlands, singing girls, and bloody noses.

Just as all was ready, an untoward event, of which no adequate explanation has ever been forthcoming, shook Athenian morale. Before the doors of most Athenian homes stood stone plinths topped by a head of Hermes, guardians of the household. In a single night, throughout the city, the Herms were mutilated by persons who must have been numerous but remained unknown. Shocked and uneasy, the Assembly invited exposure by the offer of rewards.

Nothing was vouchsafed directly about the Herms. But stories of mutilation of other statues by drunken youths, and allegations that parodies of the Eleusinian Mysteries, in which all Athenians were initiates, had been enacted at drinking parties, involved Alcibiades.

He asked for a trial before starting; it was refused from fear that the army, poised at the ready and restless at delay, would come to his support.

So on that June day, in the Peiraeus, wind lifted the Athenian sails.

At the island of Korkyra, rendezvous of the entire enterprise, there assembled 134 triremes, two 50-oared Rhodian vessels, 5,100 hoplites, many slingers and archers and one contingent of horse, plus supply ships with bakers, masons, carpenters.

157

The first setback came when this imposing force reached Italy. The cities there were unwilling to receive them. At the Straits, Rhegium would do no more than open a market outside its walls. The Athenian advance envoys returned from Segesta with only thirty talents of the promised money.

At a council of war, the three generals made characteristic proposals. Nicias urged an advance to Selinunte, to relieve the pressure on the Segestaeans, followed by a show of force to other cities in a sail-past along the coast, and then a return to Athens.

Alcibiades declared that so great an expedition could not return empty-handed. They should attack Selinunte unless it ceased its war with Segesta. They should then attack Syracuse unless it permitted restoration of the uprooted Leontinians to their homes.

> Lamachus counseled an immediate advance on Syracuse; all armies are most terrible at first. . . . Not only the sight of the armament which would never seem so numerous again, but the near approach of suffering, and above all the immediate peril of battle, would create a panic among the enemy.

Alcibiades prevailed. After a show of strength, the army, received at Naxos, settled in at Catana above Syracuse.

Meanwhile at Athens, evidence continued to be taken in the affair of the Herms. Names were named. The state ship, *Salamina*, was dispatched to bring Alcibiades and others back for trial. For form's sake, the general was not taken into custody, but allowed to follow *Salamina* in his own vessel. When they reached Thurii, he slipped away and took passage for the Peloponnese.

There, he traitorously became advisor to Sparta. He proposed a strategy that would cut off the Athenian food supply: Sparta should send troops to take and fortify Decelea in northern Attica, whence they could deny the city practically all food raised locally. Interception of the Athenian grain fleet returning from the Black Sea would then insure starvation in the city. The final battle of the Peloponnesian war, at Aegospotami in the Dardanelles, engaged and destroyed the Athenian convoy of this shipment.

Alcibiades also urged the Spartans to supply the Syracusans with a seasoned general; they sent Gylippus.

With reinforcements from the cities along the south Sicilian shore, the Syracusans moved north to attack Catana. Informed of their plans, while they were en route the Athenians sailed to the Great Harbor and got the better of an engagement there. But they were prevented from following up this advantage by Syracusan cavalry, for which they had no equivalent.

They went into winter quarters at Catana.

During the next months, both sides sought allies in the west and support from Greece. The Syracusans looked to their defenses, increased their effectiveness by reducing the number of their generals from fifteen to three.

The Athenians re-instituted hostilities by seizing the western end of the Epipolae. They built a round fort at Euryalus, and extended walls in the direction of the city.

When the Syracusans counter-attacked, Lamachus was killed. Nicias, thereby left in sole command, narrowly prevented capture of the fort by setting fire to his timber and siege engines.

The Athenian fleet advanced from Thapsos, entered the Great Harbor, invested the city. At Plemmyrium, the tip of land at the mouth of the harbor opposite Ortygia, Nicias built three forts, gained control of the passage.

But the Spartan general Gylippus had meanwhile landed at Himera and came in from the west. Crossing the Athenians' wall, he cancelled the investiture.

Nicias fell ill. He sent home a frank report of the weaknesses of the military position, and asked to be relieved. The Athenian Assembly declined to do so. Leaving him as senior officer, they dispatched two new generals, Eurymedon and Demosthenes, with a huge new expeditionary force.

Before it arrived, in the spring of 413, Gylippus took the initiative in a naval engagement in the Great Harbor. The Athenians lost only three ships to the Syracusans' eleven, but Gylippus freed the harbor passage by capturing the Plemmyrium forts. He also sent ships to Southern Italy to intercept Nicias' food supply.

Mindful of the restricted space in the Great Harbor, Gylippus redesigned his fleet, stiffening the bows of the Syracusan ships until they could be used as rams. With eighty vessels to the Athenians' seventy-five he then attacked. The engagement assumed the proportions of a rout. The Athenians' only counter-measure was to send in merchant ships with heavy pieces of iron suspended from their booms to be dropped on the Syracusan triremes.

Suddenly the opposing forces, lifting their eyes from the fighting, saw the great Athenian relief expedition sail into view: seventy-three triremes, 5,000 hoplites, numerous light troops.

The general leading it, Demosthenes, determined to execute the strategy for which Lamachus had failed to get a hearing: he attacked immediately, on land, in an effort to gain control of Euryalus and the Epipolae. Twilight came with the action still indecisive. By exception to Greek custom, he continued the engagement into the night.

Wading through moonlit haze, his troops could not distinguish friend from enemy. Because they were newly assembled from a number of cities, they were unfamiliar with those on their own side. They fought not only the enemy but each other.

160   Nor could they see the abrupt hazards of the terrain. Many fell

over the cliffs. Man after man, the Athenian army was thrown off the plateau.

Assessing this defeat, the new command counselled departure. The strategic importance of fortifying Decelea had at last been realized at Athens. They argued its priority over prolonged indecisive action in Sicily. But Nicias could not make up his mind to agree.

Illness afflicted the camp; the Athenian forces lingered in uneasy inaction.

Only when news spread that Gylippus had brought in further reinforcements did Nicias consent to go. August 28 was set as the day of departure.

On the night of August 27, the full moon entered a total eclipse. Interpreting the eerie event, the Athenian soothsayers declared no move must be made for thrice nine days. Generals and camp alike acceded.

The lull ended abruptly when the Syracusans started to build a boom from Plemmyrium to Ortygia, bottling up the harbor. Quickly manning their 110 ships, the Athenian generals urged the men to row for their lives and force a passage.

They were beaten back. Crew after panicked crew ran its craft up on the beach and sought safety with the army. Demosthenes could not get the men aboard again.

That night, the Athenians would have been able to stage an overland march to their base at Catana—the Syracusan forces had broken ranks for a stupendous celebration. But Nicias was duped into an untested conviction that the way north was blocked. Forty thousand men waited for orders. He sat out the hours until morning. By then, the blockade was real.

With no choice but to shift direction, the Athenians struck 162 westward towards Gela. Five pursued days later, their supplies totally exhausted, Demosthenes' division was surrounded. Nicias' troops, frantic for water, fought their way to the River Assinarios, where they flung themselves into the stream to gulp blood and mud while the Syracusans slaughtered them like cattle. Nicias surrendered, begged Gylippus to halt the massacre.

Gylippus intended to bring Demosthenes and Nicias back alive, but the Syracusans and Corinthians put them to death then and there. The surviving Athenian forces—7,000 men—were dumped into the stone quarries of Syracuse where for more than two months they died like flies, in blinding sun with little water. Later, the Syracusans extracted the Athenians' allies for sale as slaves, but left the Athenians and Sicilian Greeks where they were.

A few, it is said, bought their way out by reciting to culture-hungry Syracusans the tragedies of Euripides.

In Athens, the statue of Athena Nike in the exquisite small temple on the south bastion of the Acropolis looked down in irony. Completed less than twenty years, the sanctuary bore the name of Athena Apteros, the wingless victory,—wingless because the citizens of Athens had been sure that victory would never fly away.

In Syracuse, the greatest coin designers of the age, Kimon and Evaenetus, were set to work on new commemorative issues of demaretia; this time, the horses of the quadriga run at full gallop, with abandoned Athenian armor underneath their feet.

The first European empire was built by Syracuse.

CHAPTER X

The Path to Empire

With Athens eliminated as a power, Segesta, after a new dispute with Selinus, turned in the opposite direction, and in 409 successfully summoned Carthage. The Carthaginian fleet was at Motya. Hannibal the elder, grandson of the Hamilcar who died at Himera, brought a force a hundred thousand strong, marched to Selinunte, sacked it, sold the citizens into slavery, left it a stony desert.

Turning north to avenge his grandfather, at Himera he sacrificed some 3,000 men with torture to appease Hamilcar's ghost.

Panormus (Palermo) and other western cities began to mark their coinage with the mysterious Phoenician letters **ZIZ.**

Akragas was the next objective. Assisted by his cousin Himilco, Hannibal camped outside the walls, began to take stones from the Akragas cemetery to make a causeway over which to attack. A thunderbolt struck his men when they laid hands on Theron's tomb. The causeway was completed, but not with stones from the necropolis.

Plague infected the Carthaginian camp; Hannibal died. Himilco lit the fires of Moloch, sacrificed a boy.

The Akragas top command was divided between Dexippus, a Spartan general from Gela, directing the Campanian mercenaries inside the city, and Syracusan generals in charge of troops arriving from the southeast. When the latter took the hill east of town, and the Carthaginians there fled toward their main camp, a chance was missed for an intercept on the road. Seeing it, the outraged populace poured out in a futile effort to prevent reunion of the enemy forces, and subsequently stoned four of its own generals to death for their failure.

Slowly, the invested cited starved. Dexippus was bought. The hungry mercenaries transferred their allegiance to Carthage.

Philistus tells how the abandoned Akragantines "were compelled to leave, for the barbarians to pillage, those things which made their lives happy."

As Himilco's troops entered, the munificent host of the city's days of grandeur, Gellias, is said to have fled up the path to Rupe Atenea, where he placed fire on the temple platform and threw himself into the blaze.

Those who could, escaped to Gela. As the line of stripped refugees straggled away from their luxurious past, some among them may have remembered Simonides' poem:

The Path to Empire

Being but man, forbear to say
Beyond tonight what thing shall be,
And date no man's felicity.
` For know, all things
Make briefer stay
Than dragonflies, whose slender wings
Hover, and whip away.

In time to meet and halt the pursuing Carthaginians at Gela, a new tyrant arose in Syracuse.

The terms of the peace treaty made in 405 were highly favorable to the invaders. The cities they already held were recognized as subject, and Gela and Camarina as tributary, to Carthage; the Sikel communities of the interior were to be independent. But the treaty also stipulated that "the Syracusans shall be subject to Dionysius."

An interval was required to firm up his control of the city, but for thirty-eight years thereafter, Dionysius maintained himself in power. Under him, between 405 and 367 Syracuse acquired a spread of territory previously unequalled in the West.

He made the city an armed camp. Five successive gates guarded the entrance to Ortygia, now a citadel from which all but Dionysius' immediate adherents were excluded; he enlarged their ranks by mercenaries and enfranchised slaves. He permitted no independent communities closer than the Straits a hundred miles to the north: he razed Naxos, sold its inhabitants and those of Catana into slavery.

New armament, and bigger—quinquiremes instead of triremes—was made more formidable by the invention of catapults for siege warfare capable of hurling two to three hundred pound stone balls across a distance of several hundred yards. Shortly, 166 Dionysius was ready to initiate a new war.

Pushing the Carthaginians west across the island, at Motya he fought one of the most eerie engagements in history, more than fifty years in advance of its exact counterpart in Alexander the Great's capture of the Phoenicians' parent city of Tyre.

Dionysius beached his ships in the bay, set up catapults on the western shore to protect them. Himilco's fleet came in, surveyed the situation, departed. Dionysius put down rollers, trundled his ships overland northward, reappeared in the open sea. Himilco withdrew to Carthage. Dionysius turned on Motya.

The Motyans having dismantled the mole between island and shore, he constructed a new causeway. The Motyans lived in high-towered houses; he built wooden 'belfries' on wheels, rolled them across the causeway, entered the town at the height of the walls.

The battle was fought at the second storey level. House by house, the Motyans defended themselves, but Dionysius, continuing the struggle into a night lit by burning buildings, turned it into a massacre memorializing Hannibal's at Himera. He sold the surviving population, except for Greek mercenaries found fighting for Carthage. Those, he crucified.

Yet in the spring of 396, Himilco came back with power. He founded Lilybaeum (Marsala) to replace Motya. Sailing around the northwest corner of the island he successfully executed the original Punic strategy: enveloping the north coast, he reached Messana, destroyed it even to its walls. Entering Dionysius' territory, he founded Tauromenium (Taormina) as a new settlement for the Sikels. Then he moved with fleet and army on Syracuse.

Once again, Dionysius' position was imperilled by discontent within and danger without. But all armies investing Syracuse had a second enemy in the swamps around the mouth of the river Anapos; Himilco soon had to struggle against pervasive plague. It grew so bad that the dead lay unburied. In one of the night attacks which made his name terrible, Dionysius then administered a defeat that enabled him to dictate terms.

During the ensuing armistice, Dionysius conquered or made treaties with the Sikels of Morgantina, Cephalodeium (Cefalu), Enna, Centuripa. He founded Tyndaris on the north coast. But an effort to take Taormina in the dead of winter ended in his being driven down the precipitous cliffs with luck to escape alive.

War recommenced after his capture of Solus (Solunte) near Palermo. His second try at Taormina succeeded; he emptied the town and refilled it with mercenaries. All the Greek and Sikel communities of Sicily were now in his power. His new tremendous walls at Fort Euryalus and around the Epipolae remain as records of the best in fourth century Greek military architecture.

Expanding into Italy, Dionysius made Lokri his main base and ally. The choice was in part because of its proximity to Rhegium, for which he felt special enmity—when he had sent there asking for a Rhegine wife, the reply had indicated that only the hangman's daughter was available. By 387, he held Rhegium; with his capture of Croton two years later, he became the most powerful ruler in Southern Italy.

On both sides of the Adriatic, all the way up to Hadria (Venice), his entrepot that was the Hellenic world's northern outpost, he established colonies or alliances—that with King Alcetas of Molossia (the present Albanian and Greek Epirus) gave him a foothold on the Greek mainland. Observing his rise, the Athenians sought to replace the Spartans as his ally. In 368, they succeeded. Dominion as broad as his was a new phenomenon in European history.

Yet Dionysius never controlled all of Sicily. During two more Carthaginian wars he traded blows, with the line of demarcation shifting back and forth between east and west. Victory took him all the way to Eryx, but defeat soon threw him back again.

168

Just after this rebuff, news came of the success of his tragedy, *The Ransom of Hector,* in the annual competition at Athens' Lenaean festival. In view of the repeated failures of his previous entries, it was perhaps not a coincidence that the award was made the year he signed a treaty with Athens. He died as a result of over-celebration.

Dionysius' minister Dion was his brother-in-law, his son-in-law and his successor. A philosopher as well, he hoped so to mould Dionysius' son, Dionysius II, as to eliminate tyranny from the government. He importuned Plato to come to Syracuse to engage in the enterprise.

Plato was reluctant. He had been in Syracuse in 388, during Dionysius I's time, and left with fixed convictions about the iniquities of tyranny—the tyrant, tiring of him, had ordered him sold as a slave, and he had escaped only through the prompt and skilled aid of friends. But he agreed to return.

The new experiment was a failure. At first, Dionysius II was amenable to Plato's teaching, but the philosopher was not content with superficial progress, and insisted that the young ruler acquire grounding that was truly firm. He says in his *Letters:*

> When I had arrived, I thought I ought first to put it to the proof whether Dionysius was really all on fire with philosophy or whether the frequent reports that had come to Athens to that effect amounted to nothing. Now there is an experimental method for determining the truth in such cases that, far from being vulgar, is truly appropriate to despots, especially those stuffed with second-hand opinions, which I perceived, as soon as I arrived, was very much the case with Dionysius. One must point out to such men that the whole plan is possible and explain what preliminary steps and how much hard work it will require, for the hearer, if he is genuinely devoted to philosophy and is a man of God with a natural affinity and fitness

169

for the work, sees in the course marked out a path of enchantment, which he must at once strain every nerve to follow, or die in the attempt. . . .

As for those, however, who are not genuine converts to philosophy, but have only a superficial tinge of doctrine—like the coat of tan that people get in the sun—as soon as they see how many subjects there are to study, how much hard work they involve, and how indispensable it is for the project to adopt a well-ordered scheme of living, they decide that the plan is difficult if not impossible for them, and so they really do not prove capable of practising philosophy.

Cursory travel along Plato's path left Dionysius II disenchanted. Discipline irked him—he had been held on a tight rein by his father, and proposed to enjoy himself now his father was gone. Their relations are made graphic by a story of a verbal exchange after the young man had seduced a married woman:

Dionysius II: "It is well for you to chide me, but you did not have a tyrant for a father."

Dionysius I: "And if you go on doing this sort of thing, you will not have a tyrant for a son."

Furthermore, a court duel was in process between history and philosophy. The wealthy historian Philistus had been Dionysius I's sponsor in his first appeal for power. The Assembly assessed a fine against any speaker who spoke provocatively; every time that Dionysius I incurred it, in the harangue that obtained authorization for him to become tyrant, Philistus announced his willingness to pay, and thereby enabled his protégé to complete his appeal. Later, Dionysius I exiled Philistus, who wrote his *History* while rusticating at an Adriatic outpost, but now he was back, heading a faction favorable to continuation of the tyranny, and undermining Dion.

The majority of Plato's surviving *Letters* are either to or about Dionysius; they describe the philosopher's successive attempts to develop a philosopher-king in the flesh. The details of his frustrations go far toward explaining why the political system of his later years posited ideal rulers.

Yet in 361 Plato undertook still another journey to Sicily, in an effort to mediate when Dionysius II fell out with Dion. This mission too was unsuccessful. Thereafter, Dion was murdered. Plato's long *Seventh Letter*, "To the friends and companions of Dion," reviews his entire experience at Syracuse.

These mid-century years of struggle between Dion and Dionysius II left the city torn and miserable: some of the citizens finally appealed to the Corinthians to supply a new ruler. They sent Timoleon.

He was given the assignment as a moral test: he had saved his brother's life in battle, but when the brother tried to make himself tyrant, had acquiesced in his death. The Corinthians, divided as to whether he was a fratricide or a hero, declared his record at Syracuse should be regarded as his trial.

Plutarch states that his omens were auspicious from the start: when he sailed for Syracuse in 344, he was guided by a torch in the sky, symbol of Demeter and Persephone. On his arrival, Hadranus, the Sikel god of Aetna, indicated approval, and Dionysius II agreed to surrender Ortygia if allowed to retire to Corinth.

Timoleon dismantled the island stronghold. He destroyed all monuments that might induce the revival of factions, including Dionysius I's tomb, leaving only Gelon's statue. He summoned thousands of new settlers to stabilize the city's population of mer- *171* cenaries and uprooted peoples. He revived the laws of Diocles, instituted a new democracy with government in the hands of an annually elected priest of Zeus. For twenty years, popular government survived at Syracuse.

In the north at Tyndaris, in the south at newly refounded Gela, Timoleon built walls which remain as monuments to the scale of his military strategy, even though in his time they were unused.

The auspices were good again when in 339 Timoleon defeated a tremendous Carthaginian force arriving for a new invasion. The Greek army, advancing to an encounter at the Crimisos river near Segesta, was dismayed to meet on the road a mule train laden with selinon, for they used the plant to wreath sepulchral slabs. Timoleon quickly explained that Corinthians plaited this plant into crowns for winners at the Isthmian Games. He wreathed his own head, and at that moment two eagles appeared, one bearing a serpent. Exalted as they had been downcast, the Greeks joined battle. A thunder-and-hail storm broke in the Carthaginians' faces. The suddenly swollen river swept hundreds of them away.

As a measure of pacification, this victory ranked with the first Himera. Timoleon sent the choicest of its spoils to be dedicated in Poseidon's temple at the Isthmus.

His trial by ordeal having clearly proved him a hero, Timoleon retired to land given him by the grateful Syracusans; after his death, he was venerated in the Timoleonteion—a colonnaded gymnasium near the Temple of Zeus on the shores of the Great Harbor. Had Plato lived to see Syracuse under Timoleon's leadership he might have thought ideal philosopher-kings could exist in the flesh after all.

By 317, however, Syracuse was again a kingly tyranny under 172 Agathocles, who carried the next war with Carthage to North

Africa and raised a siege of Syracuse by operations based on Cap
Bon.

Wide-sweeping empires were on the make everywhere: King
Philip II of Macedon had obtained control of all Greece in 338
and his son Alexander had led a victorious army all the way to
India and was sighing for new worlds to conquer when he died
at Babylon in 323. His successor-generals, in Egypt and around
the shores of the Middle East, were taking the name of kings.
Agathocles' third wife was the daughter of Ptolemy I of Egypt;
his daughter married King Pyrrhus of Epirus.

Pyrrhus received his military training under Alexander the
Great; when asked which of the young men was the best, Alexander's ranking commander replied: "Pyrrhus, if he lives to be
old." Hannibal the younger classed him with Alexander.

He crossed the Adriatic to Italy at the invitation of the Taran-
tines, who were seeking to balance nearby Thurii's alliance with

the rising power of Rome. The cost of his victories has become axiomatic. Partly because of fright at the elephants he had brought from Asia, the Romans lost 7,000 men when he fought them at Heraclea in 280, but his own losses were so great that Pyrrhus is alleged to have said, "Another victory of this kind and I shall return alone to Epirus."

He went to Sicily, with the intention of clearing the island of Carthaginians, but their persistent stand at Lilybaeum exhausted his patience. In 275 he returned to Epirus, saying of Magna Graecia, "My friends, what a wrestling ground for Carthaginians and Romans we are leaving behind us!"

The implied eclipse of Greek independence came quickly in Southern Italy: Rome controlled the entire peninsula by 272.

Next, Rome became a Sicilian power by absorbing the Campanian mercenaries known as Mammertines, "sons of Mars," who had settled at Messana, and its first war with Carthage ended in the transfer of all of Sicily except Syracuse to Roman rule as Rome's first province.

Syracuse enjoyed a final half century of self-government under a general who in 265 became king as Hieron II and insured his independence by making a treaty with the Romans and supplying them with naval stores and grain.

In this twilight interval, Hieron developed a tax system, equitably based on tithing, that Rome later extended over the whole island. He embellished the city with new buildings. The theater took on much the shape it bears today, its seat-groups identified by the names of Zeus Olympios, Herakles the Benevolent, and those of himself, Philistis his wife, and Nereis, his daughter-in-law. In the Neapolis area, he dedicated a great new altar some six hundred fifty feet in length to Zeus Eleutherios (the liberator). New doors to the temple of Athena were made of ivory with gold knobs. Paintings of Agathocles' victories frescoed its walls. Cicero said:

> You will often have been told that Syracuse is the largest of Greek cities and the loveliest of all cities. Gentlemen, what you have been told is true.

At this time, Sicilian patrons of the arts assembled collections of the best of all periods of classic Greek sculpture: one Messanian collector, Gaius Heius, is said to have possessed an Eros by Praxiteles, a Herakles by Myron and two bronze maidens bearing baskets by Polykleitos. This was when Theocritus composed his idylls, *177*

when the Venus Landolina of the Syracuse Museum was carved, when science prospered under Archimedes.

Archimedes was a native Syracusan, and may have been a relative of Hieron; at least, a number of stories of his major discoveries in physics concern the king. When Hieron fretted lest his golden crown contain silver alloy, Archimedes compared the displacement of the crown in water against that of its weight in pure gold. The idea is said to have come to him when he observed his own displacement in the public bath—shouting "Eureka!" ("I've found it!") he raced home naked through the street to test his inspiration.

His development of the use of the lever—"Give me a place to stand and I will move the earth"—is said to have been tested by Hieron himself; Archimedes enabled his king to lift a fully laden ship.

Preoccupied with physics and mathematics, he yielded unwillingly when Hieron urged him to put his discoveries to useful ends, but he developed the water screw for bailing boats and for irrigation, and the concave mirror for starting fires (said to have been used on Punic shipping); and he greatly strengthened the Syracusan defenses.

These were tested after Hannibal the younger, arriving with his elephants via Spain and the passes of the Alps, inflicted his imposing defeat on Rome at Cannae in the Second Punic War. Viewing the debacle, Hieron II's successors underwent doubts as to the wisdom of their Roman alliance. Soon, a powerful Syracusan faction suggested a change of sides. Hieron's son Hieronymus defected. The Roman proconsul of the rest of the island, M. Claudius Marcellus, determined to incorporate Syracuse into his province, and marched against the city in 213.

Archimedes' defenses held. Marcellus entered only after treachery had opened a gate. His troops found Archimedes working on a problem. Against orders, they killed him as he worked.

His tomb was marked by a sphere inscribed in a cylinder—one of his more important propositions had demonstrated the relation between the two. Later, Cicero found the grave overgrown with brambles and saved it from oblivion:

Thus would this most famous and once most learned city of Greece have remained a stranger to the tomb of one of its most ingenious citizens.

Roman Sicily produced little history, though in 36 B.C. when Pompey's son Sextus seized the island Agrippa landed at Tyndaris and Octavian at Naxos in the campaign to throw him out. A provincial granary, it was farmed by slave labor and troubled by periodic slave revolts—the slave leader of the First Servile War controlled a territory comprising Taormina, Catana, Enna and Akragas.

In many cities—the best example is Taormina—the Romans turned existing theaters into amphitheaters for their gladiatorial contests and fights between wild beasts. Elsewhere they built new arenas especially for the purpose, as at Paestum, Catana, Syracuse. Some of the amphitheaters could be flooded for combats between crocodiles and men in boats.

Roman arches, as in the gymnasium at Tyndaris, witness their expansion of a number of existing settlements; the Odeon at Taormina and the theater at Tyndari are Roman, and so is most of Solunte near Palermo. A magnificent Roman sarcophagus, carved with the story of Phaedra and Hippolytus, is preserved in the Cathedral Museum at Akragas.

But of all the Roman remains on the island, easily the most conspicuous is the stately pleasure dome erected sometime in the course of the 4th century A.D. at Casale, near Piazza Armerina in the mountains southeast of Enna. Its acres of mosaics are now preserved under the glass of what looks like a giant Victorian conservatory. Vast scenes of hunts, processions, the occupations of the agricultural year, men and ships, domestic animals, and wild beasts from the whole known world floor room after room in colorful profusion.

The owner of the palace is uncertain; perhaps it was the retirement villa of the Emperor Maximianus, whose son Maxentius lost his life challenging Constantine's supremacy and whose daughter Fausta became Constantine's wife. That the villa was used long enough to go through successive redecorations is proved by the floor of a room where an early geometrically patterned mosaic has been plastered over and replaced by a scene more to later taste, displaying six girl athletes in bikinis.

The Roman event of most pertinence to Greek antiquity in the island remains the trial of Verres. This official's callous rapacity forecast treatment that Sicilians have since undergone at many hands. By giving the provenance of what the governor stole, Cicero supplies an astonishingly complete inventory of the moveable artistic wealth accumulated during the centuries when Greeks dwelt in independent communities in Sicily.

CHAPTER XI

Figures of Later Legend

Just as the singers of myths of gods and heroes and the great epics of Troy transmitted stories with scenes in Italy and Sicily to the Western Greeks, later story-tellers transmitted accounts of Moors and paladins, of chivalry and Christendom. Graphic and performing arts made them familiar alike to illiterate peasant, landowner and overlord. They are still familiar today.

These transmitters—painters of Sicilian carts, puppeteers, itinerant singers—worked, and still work, in humble media. Yet in exactitude their art is as demanding as the phrasing of hexameters.

In the museum of folk art at Palermo, in the Palazzo Corvaia   *183*

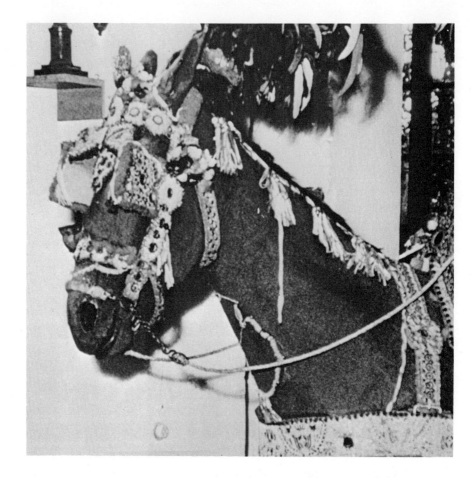

at Taormina, are painted carts whose freshness is like that of the varnished sleighs in exhibits of early Americana. Dimming panels from long-dismantled vehicles hang for sale outside Sicilian antique shops, like the occasional Conestoga wagon attracting buyers alongside an American highway.

But the painted cart is not yet obsolete. Possession of such a cart remains a goal of many a Sicilian peasant family. Their main means of transport, it is used for agricultural hauling of all sorts and out in all weather. Its colors eventually blur. But particularly

in eastern Sicily, great numbers of quick little horses or sad little donkeys, with bell-stands dingling above their belly-bands and wisps of colored cloth on their headstalls, go about country or city errands as gaily decorated as their accompanying masters are drably clad.

Every inch of a cart is painted with minute care—tiny designs circle the wheel rims, run up the spokes to hubs that, like the undercarriage, are often further embellished with patterned metal. The big scenes are on the large panels forming the body of the cart and its tail-gate. Splendid knights and paladins go forth to the Crusades. In bloody combat, the dread Moor is vanquished. St. George pierces the dragon with cunning skill as his charger rears back, stiff-legged from lash of scaly tail, wild-eyed from fire of flaming nostrils.

Carts are still made in various places: Aci Sant' Antonio on the east coast between Catania and Taormina specializes in their production. Traditional panel scenes are sufficiently numerous to afford choice—the patterns are not nearly as limited as those, say, on painted wagons in the area around Thessalonika in Greece. Yet the traditional presentation must be—and is—seriously observed. Twentieth century schmaltz may appear occasionally on the bows of boats in harbors fancied by the tourist trade, but the carts preserve the ritual dignity of the primitive agricultural year.

On feast days, one may come upon a cart that is kept for special occasions. On Easter Monday, in Palermo, when the waterfront fair was drawing to a close and homebound families were piled, literally by the dozen, in every available horse-drawn taxi-carriage, I saw the littlest donkey ever, wearing every possible adornment including a very tall orange cockade, and drawing a bandbox-fresh cart. The owner, a bulging individual of at least two hundred and thirty pounds, could hardly plump himself down on the

cart without spilling over. Man and beast clearly enjoyed the attention they attracted.

But if the painted cart is a continuing transmitter of the days of chivalry, the Sicilian puppet has his back to the wall. Since the war, the number of puppet theaters has dwindled until no more

than two or three are active in Palermo and its environs, where as many as forty-five prospered at the beginning of this century, and the situation is the same in Catania.

The puppets from these two cities differ greatly in size: the Palermo type, though itself larger than most Western puppets, comes about to the thigh of the operator, while the much larger Catanian type often stands two-thirds of the height of the man who manipulates it. Both have in common their beautiful silk garments and hand-wrought armor, sometimes of brass and tin but often of copper and silver. Visors of their plumed helmets are closed with decisive gestures when a fight is in the offing; their shields, embossed, like their greaves, with each particular knight's own device, are raised in readiness; swords are drawn in preparation for sword-play and footwork that would credit any human 188 fencer.

A puppet stage is usually divided into two or three zones, at each side of which an operator stands in the wings. Sicilian puppets are operated not only with the strings attached to the less essential parts of their anatomy, but with iron rods. One of these is attached to the head, with a hook at the top that permits suspension from a chain when the puppet is on stage but not in action. The other connects with the puppet's good right arm: a fight thus becomes a duel between two operators holding rigid weapons. Whether the contest be between Christian and Moor, Knight and Dragon, Champion and Giant, it is fought with strength and stamina; when it is over, fragments of armor and bodies often litter the stage floor.

Aficionado audiences strictly require exact observance of classical presentation and classical scripts. Script books, in beautiful and often faded handwriting, usually hang at the side of the stage, and a collection of texts, *Storia dei Paladini di Francia*, was published in Palermo in 1896. But the puppeteers and the elderly men who with a scattering of tourists make up today's audiences know the lines by heart. The plays are divided into seven major cycles, comprising enough separate episodes for some seven hundred performances: Constantine the Great; the Kings of France; Charlemagne and the French Paladins, including Rinaldo and Orlando at Roncesvalles; the Holy Grail; the Adventures of the Brothers Dolores and Staniero; Orlando in Search of the Grail; the Liberation of Jerusalem.

Painted banner-signs, with a dozen or more scenes from a given cycle in two rows down their length, illustrate the stories and serve as playbills; they decorate the walls of the theater or are hung out in front to attract trade. A puppeteer may own as many as sixty sign-panels, a hundred backdrops and flys, and anywhere from 60 to 100 puppets, with ample supplies of extra heads.

Sometimes two puppets play successive scenes in a single part. In the Catanian cast of Salvatore Macrì, the son of Emanuele Macrì of Acireale now in the United States, one beautiful Rinaldo is used up to the final episode in which the hero winds his horn when it is too late. A second is substituted for the death scene; it is identical in form and costume, but with a tube alongside the rod attached to his head through which lifelike-looking blood flows from eyes, nose and mouth. (In other casts, the head of the puppet is changed between acts.) In this same collection there is a tube in the head of the hundred pound green dragon through which it breathes out smoke as St. George approaches.

Among favorite characters, Perinda, the female warrior, has many devotees. On one occasion, she fights and vanquishes a Moor. In Palermo puppet casts, Moors never have names, though in Catanian casts they are endowed with resounding ones. Another brilliant performer is Achille, who comes from Siberia but is the son of a Christian. Giuseppe Argenti, whose theater operates in the Via Pappagallo (the Street of the Parrot) in Palermo, regards his Achille as the most beautiful of his collection. But choice is difficult in a row that includes a slant-eyed Oriental whom Marco Polo might have brought back with him, Pope Gregory IV with bishop's crook and mitre ready to bless departing Crusaders, and a Programmist in eighteenth century dress who comes before the curtain to announce the evening's episodes.

Yet today, many puppeteers with long family traditions in the art are seeking their living elsewhere. The puppets of a number of theaters dangle unemployed from the ceiling of their owners' homes. Others come into the market singly, for sale by antique dealers. Admissions from such tourists as persist until they locate the little theaters on the back streets and from the old men in the neighborhood who come night after night on weekly or monthly

subscriptions are not enough to keep a puppeteering family going, and the Sicilian tourist authorities seem unaware of this beautiful but wasting asset.

The stories the puppets act out, however, are not being entirely forgotten, for in spoken form they are carried around the country by itinerant singers. In Agrigento, I listened to Rifini the Great. A sign mounted on the top of his little car is a travelling advertisement. Inside the car is a huge canvas roll on which some twenty numbered scenes are painted; unfurled, it serves both as a backdrop to his performance and a program of his repertoire, legible to illiterate and literate alike. A microphone on a cord long enough to permit dancing, a loudspeaker cone, a record player and a long pointer complete the props that he brings out in town squares at the luncheon interval.

Announcing a request number, he indicates the appropriate picture with his pointer and starts to sing the story into the mike. From time to time, he rests his voice by putting on the record while he dances, but at climaxes, when the hero is in real danger, the news is carried live. A collection plate circulated by a colleague supports the show; the crowd clusters like swarming bees.

The paladins celebrated in these stories have left further evidence behind. Even if the visitor in search of Greek sites were a single-minded and highly selective purist, he could hardly ignore the landscape created by real-life Moors, Crusaders and other conquerors and their stories in medieval Italy and Sicily.

During the eighth to tenth centuries, the Arab conquest of North Africa was extended into Spain and Sicily. Enna fell in 859. From Constantinople, the Byzantine emperors attempted to stay the tide, but Syracuse was lost in 878 and Taormina in 902. At Mount Eryx, the castle ruins include the stone columbarium for

the carrier pigeons by which the Moors maintained rapid communication with North Africa. Widespread Arab immigration brought in Arab culture.

Then in 1038 the Byzantines came back. An expedition under General George Maniaces regained the east coast from Messina to Syracuse. The general built a castle at the tip of Ortygia, bringing entire rooms from Constantinople to embellish the interior. He adorned the exterior with two finely-worked antique bronze rams that turned with the wind and bleated when it blew. One of them has survived and chews a thoughtful cud in the Palermo Museum; the other was destroyed in the revolution of 1848.

Among Maniaces' mercenaries were two sons of a sturdy and prolific Viking, Tancred de Hauteville, who lived near Coutances in Normandy. Several of this restless Norseman's twelve boys had

sought their fortunes further south. When Maniaces was recalled to Byzantium, Pope Nicholas II conceived the design of diverting Sicilian allegiance to the west. He commissioned Tancred's son Robert Guiscard, already well established in south-central Italy, to extend his holdings. Robert's oath of allegiance ran, "by the grace of God and St. Peter duke of Apulia and Calabria and, with their help, hereafter of Sicily."

With the blessing of the pope and the aid of Arab dissensions, Duke Robert and his brother, Count Roger, who did most of the fighting, advanced to Enna, took Palermo in 1072. The conquest of the island was complete by the end of the century.

Under Roger I and his son Roger II, who united all Norman possessions in Italy, Sicily and North Africa and even undertook forays into the Greek empire, Sicily rapidly developed as cosmopolitan a culture as Western Europe had ever known.

The Norman chancery issued its official texts in Latin, Arabic, Greek. Roger's civil service included Byzantine lawyers, Arab fiscal experts. Like the Arabs before them, the Normans practised religious toleration. Successive Norman archbishops of Palermo were a Greek ecclesiastic, Nicodemus; a Frenchman, Stephen of Perche; and an Englishman, Walter of the Mill.

Roger II's chief admiral, Giorgio d'Antiocha, was a Syro-Greek who came to Palermo in 1112. An Orthodox Christian, he built the Martorana, the church that even today is more often known as Santa Maria dell'Ammiraglio, and that displays, among its superb mosaics, the patron offering the building to the Virgin. Under Roger's patronage, the Spanish Arab Edrisi produced an epoch-making geographic work. Roger brought jongleurs from France, moved Vergil's body from Posilippo to the Castel del 'Uova in Naples to permit wider veneration.

196   The indefatigable Norman urge to build, that remade skylines

from Durham Cathedral in northern England to the Krak des
Chevaliers at Acre in Asia Minor was never and nowhere more
lavishly satisfied than in the south Italian and Sicilian outthrust
contemporary with the cross-Channel move of William the Con-
queror.

It combined all the culture's diverse elements. Cathedral exteriors that if not fronted by palm trees would fit with contemporary structures at Ely or Albi have marble inner walls inlaid below with geometric Arab designs and adorned above with Byzantine mosaics comparable to those at Daphni in Greece or Hagia Sophia in Constantinople.

Roger II enlarged the Palazzo Reale that the Arabs had begun in the 9th century. Horsemen could ride abreast up the monumental marble stair that spirals around the central courtyard.

In the Cappella Palatina, the King's private sanctuary, the blue and gold mosaics, when illumined by streaks of sunlight through clerestory windows and the candles of an Easter mass, gleam in sapphire-and-topaz as brilliant as the sapphire-and-ruby when Parisian sun pours through the windows of the Sainte Chapelle. The walls of his private apartments, the Sala di Re Ruggero, are likewise covered with mosaics, secular representations of peacocks, wild animals, hunts. The nearby church of San Giovanni degli Eremite, founded by Pope Gregory the Great in Roger II's time, has a cloister in which slender Arabic double columns support Norman arches through which can be glimpsed the pink Byzantine domes of a church one part of which was originally a mosque.

Roger's churches included the great Norman cathedral at Cefalu, the headland east of Palermo that resembles the profile of a man. When caught off the north coast in one of the sudden squalls that make small boats ungovernable, he promised a cathedral as a votive if he should be helped to reach land. The exterior of the tremendous church is pure Norman; the opulence of the interior mosaics illustrates why Amari called Roger a "baptised sultan." In the apse is a mighty Christ Pantocrator; on the walls are imposing apostles and bishops. Most arresting of all are the

tetramorphs—representations of the heads of the four apocalyptic beings, surrounded by huge wings, on wheels.

Roger II was crowned on Christmas Day, 1130, in the Palermo cathedral, in whose somewhat bleak interior he and subsequent royalty lie, some in wall-tombs and others under columned canopies, in heavy porphyry supported by pompous lions. The Cathedral's superb Norman exterior is afflicted by a highly extraneous Renaissance dome, an architectural olisthostroma. Roger II was succeeded by his son William the Bad, a creature of his prime minister Majone, who dabbled in astrology but also erected the Moorish Church of San Cataldo.

The great cathedral at Monreale on Mount Caputo outside the city overlooking the Conca d'Oro was founded by Roger's grand-son, William the Good, whom a contemporary memorialized as

"Rex ille magnifico, cujus vita placuit Deo et hominibus." Its tremendous bronze doors were sculptured by Bonanno of Pisa. Inside and out, it assembles all the gifts brought to this crossroads of architectural style. Some of the double columns upholding the arches of the cloister are carved with the Norman zigzag, some inlaid in Arabic mosaic; their capitals include scenes with persons, floral designs, a delightful owl. The fountain in one corner has a Pompeian basin at its base; a column carved in zigzag rises from its center; Bacchantes dance around the issuing water at its top.

The mosaics of Monreale's huge interior are in browns and tans. A Pantocrator looks awesomely down from the dome above the

transept. In the apse, beside a Christ that recalls those of the Cappella Palatina and Cefalu, "I am the light of the world" appears in both Greek and Latin. The upper walls of the nave, marbled below, portray Old Testament episodes. The tempo of these visual accounts is delightfully tranquil. Instead of representations of one scene from each of many stories, sequences show step-by-step such episodes as the Fall of Man, until Adam and Eve leave the garden comfortably swathed in fleecy sheepskins. The building of the Ark ignores none of its problems, including the swinging of a complete roof into place by block and tackle. In mosaic, above the royal throne on the right of the transept, William receives his crown directly from Christ; above the bishop's throne on the left, he presents the cathedral.

Both of the Williams built pleasure palaces as well as churches: William I started the Moorish Zisa (from the Arabic aziz, magnificent); William II the Cuba (from the Arabic Kubbeh, dome) near the Palazzo Reale, and the little Cubola.

When William II died childless, a contest for the succession brought Tancred, an illegitimate grandson of Roger II, into brief authority, but when he died his seven-year-old son was dispossessed in favor of the rights of William's aunt Constance. In 1186, she had married the German Hohenstaufen prince, Henry VI, son of Barbarossa and already the holder of substantial Italian territories. Henry came to Sicily to claim this heritage and was crowned in Palermo on the day that Constance, left behind in Germany, bore his son, Frederick II.

Fatherless at three and orphaned the next year, Frederick was brought up in Sicily as the ward of Pope Innocent III. When the

brilliant, multilingual, multicultural lad was fourteen, the Pope wrote of him, "As was said of the Caesars, his peers, power comes before its time, and from the door of puberty with swift steps he enters the years of discretion and with his powers anticipates the years."

Though his life was lived in the early thirteenth century, this was a Renaissance man: Elizabeth Tudor would have understood him well. The sonnet was invented at his court in 1233. He founded the universities of Padua and Naples. Dante regarded him as the father of Italian poetry.

An administrator, he established King's judges to replace baronial courts, and a parliament which included two wise men from each demesne town, drawn from the third estate. A negotiator with excellent relations among the Arabs, when Papal prodding finally forced him to undertake a long-deferred Crusade, he achieved his purposes bloodlessly, securing Jerusalem, Bethlehem and Nazareth by treaty.

A builder, he erected many castles in Italy, among them the superb Castel del Monte near Barletta; in Sicily, new or enlarged structures dotted the island from Trapani to Syracuse, including a twenty-four tower stronghold at Enna, where he held his parliament, and the lava-walled Castello Ursino at Catania, forbidding without and delicately grooved of arch within.

Like Elizabeth's, Frederick II's theory of royal administration was to keep his entourage revolving in constant splendor around the land. The massive caravans of his court, the nobles and high officials on their horses, the curtained litters of his harem guarded by eunuch outriders, the musicians, the clerks, the records, the baggage and supply trains, as they wound up and down the precipitous roads from city to city, must have been even more cumbersome than the vehicles of an Elizabethan Progress. Biagio d'Antonio da Firenze's painting, *The Triumph of Scipio Africanus,* could well be a portrait of this court en route.

A sportsman and horse fancier, Frederick himself wrote a profusely illuminated treatise on falconry, *De Arte Venandi cum Avibus,* still in print, whose manuscript is one of the treasures of the Vatican Library. Prior to his time, the hooding of falcons was unknown in the west; he introduced it from Arab practices. He likewise ordered written a compendium, *De Medicina Equorum,* on veterinary lore.

Again like a Tudor, Frederick had four wives, unnumbered mistresses, and when he died left a problem of succession. One of the most romantic figures of history, the hero of Byron's drama *Manfred,* was his son by his mistress Bianca Lancia; the youth was crowned king of Sicily and Calabria in 1258 but Pope Urban IV excommunicated him as a usurper and he fell in battle defending his rights against his papally favored replacement Charles of Anjou.

Twenty-four years later, popular grievance against the Angevin dynasty erupted in the savage violence of the Sicilian Vespers. On Easter Tuesday 1282, as worshippers emerged from the church of San Spiritu on the eastern outskirts of Palermo, a French soldier made an insulting comment on a girl. It set off a spontaneous slaughter that spread like wind-blown fire. Before the Vespers ended, hundreds on hundreds of Frenchmen had been hunted down in a night of bloody knives.

When it was over, Sicily was again in search of a ruler. Manfred's son-in-law, Peter of Aragon, was accepted, and for four hundred and thirty years, Spanish rulers reigned and their viceroys governed Sicily. The island's great Renaissance and baroque structures date from this period.

The territorial exchanges of the Peace of Utrecht produced new uncertainties; by 1735 the Bourbon Don Carlos was settled in Na-

ples as King of the Two Sicilies, Sicily-beyond-the-lighthouse and Sicily-this-side-of-the-lighthouse, the lighthouse being that at the Straits of Messina.

After a century and a quarter of Bourbon dominance, Gladstone castigated the regime as "the negation of God erected into a system of government," and Garibaldi, landing at Marsala, began in Sicily the revolution that brought Victor Emmanuel to the throne as a constitutional monarch and united the island and the whole Italian peninsula.

Beneath its formal rule, particularly in the western part of the island, Sicily has for generations also had its shadow government, the Mafia. From the days of the Roman latifundia—large farms worked by slave labor—much of the fertile land of Sicily has been mishandled, with absentee landlords living it up in Rome, while thug overseers alternately or simultaneously squeezed the tenants below and cheated the owners above them, to the degradation of the economic level at which all but a few Sicilians lived. Since the war, however, particularly in the central and eastern parts of the island, industrial development—oil and electricity, for example—has been stimulated by public investment through the Fund for the South, and by in-migration of plants from other parts of Italy induced by tax concessions. At the same time, pressure on resources has been lessened, and island income increased, by out-migration to productive centers of the European Common Market by workers who send home part of their pay.

In a single day, I saw both Sicilies. On the facing benches of a third-class train carriage, I sat knee-to-knee with a young woman. In worn and rusty black, she looked already old. She held a baby; the nylon blanket wrapping it was new. The baby was dying. Poison from a septic ear had entered the blood-stream; it had even ceased to cry.

When she looked up, her bitter and desperate face was like that of a cornered vixen. When she looked down, her anguish softened into heart-rending tenderness. I thought of the second act of Gian-Carlo Menotti's *Consul*.

Toward the end of that day, I left the train at a way-station and fell into conversation with the station master. He summoned his wife; as we talked I sensed that both were happily expecting someone. Another train rolled in, and she was on it. Their daughter. With pride, they presented her, a law student at the University of Catania.

In the surrounding villages, when on chilly afternoons the women of the family bring their straight little wooden chairs out-of-doors to warm themselves in the sun, an unmarried girl will be thought almost unmarriageably bold unless she sets her chair to face the wall. Yet here was a girl—perhaps the station master and his wife had been denied a son—who was being given a chance. I congratulated all three. As I left, they made me a present of their own blood oranges, nourished from Aetna's life-giving lava.

APPENDIX

LIST OF ILLUSTRATIONS

213

List of Illustrations

214

List of Illustrations

°courtesy Ashmolean Museum, Oxford
†courtesy Museum of Fine Arts, Boston
all other photographs by the author

INDEX

Index